D1055479

# GOLF*Skills*

# GOLF*Skills*

Mel Sole and John Ledesma

THUNDER BAY
P · R · E · S · S
San Diego, California

## Thunder Bay Press

An imprint of the Advantage Publishers Group
5880 Oberlin Drive, San Diego, CA 92121-4794
www.thunderbaybooks.com

Produced by PRC Publishing Ltd.
64 Brewery Road, London N7 9NT, England

A member of **Chrysalis** Books plc

All notations of errors or omissions should be addressed to Thunder Bay Press, Editorial Department, at the above address. All other correspondence (author inquiries, permissions) concerning the content of this book should be addressed to PRC Publishing Ltd, 64 Brewery Road, London N7 9NT, England.

ISBN 1-59223-091-1

Library of Congress Cataloging-in-Publication Data available on request.

Printed and bound in Malaysia

1 2 3 4 5  07 06 05 04 03


ACKNOWLEDGMENTS
The publisher wishes to thank Simon Clay for taking all the photography in this book. The illustrations were supplied by Kang Chen (© PRC Publishing).

All photography is copyright © Chrysalis Images.

For front and back cover photo credits, please see jacket.

# CONTENTS

INTRODUCTION . . . . . . . . . . . . . . . . . . . . . .6

MASTERING THE BASICS . . . . . . . . . . . . .16

THE SWING . . . . . . . . . . . . . . . . . . . . . .46

WOOD PLAY . . . . . . . . . . . . . . . . . . . . . .70

IRON PLAY . . . . . . . . . . . . . . . . . . . . . .78

PITCHING . . . . . . . . . . . . . . . . . . . . . . .84

CHIPPING . . . . . . . . . . . . . . . . . . . . . .100

PUTTING . . . . . . . . . . . . . . . . . . . . . . .114

SAND PLAY . . . . . . . . . . . . . . . . . . . . .138

HAZARDS AND TROUBLE SHOTS . . . . . . .162

PROBLEM SOLVING . . . . . . . . . . . . . . . .190

COURSE MANAGEMENT . . . . . . . . . . . . .238

MENTAL ATTITUDE . . . . . . . . . . . . . . . .242

INDEX . . . . . . . . . . . . . . . . . . . . . . . . .254

# INTRODUCTION

Some golfers take their improvement more seriously than others, but every golfer wants to get better. You may hit only one or two good shots during your entire round, but the pursuit of more keeps you coming back. Golf is a game of perfection that can never be perfected. You won't come across a great number of ex-golfers. It seems that anyone who's ever picked up the sticks is hooked for life.

There are various methods for improving your game. You can pick up one of the endless offerings in golf instruction magazines, videos, CD-roms, or related media. You can plan marathon sessions in front of the tube watching the Golf Channel. You can purchase any of the miracle golf clubs or training aids advertised ad nauseam. And if you're serious about playing better golf, we strongly recommend that you be evaluated by a PGA professional. However, for those without the time and cash to attend golf school, *Golf Skills* will offer the reader the book equivalent to lessons from a professional golfer.

GOLF SKILLS

That being said, there is no one way to swing a golf club. There are multitudes of wrong ways, but there is no absolute right way. Avoid an instructor who tells you otherwise. A good instructor is one that will work with what you have. If someone tells you he or she intends to overhaul your entire swing, grab your bag and run. A good golf teacher will ask you questions before they start giving instructions. A good golf teacher makes you feel comfortable and is aware of your goals. Not everyone is aiming to be a scratch player; some simply want to shave a few strokes. A good teacher will approach each individual differently.

Evidence of golf swing differences is on display each week at any professional tournament. Atop the leaderboard, you'll find many excellent players shooting well under par and not one of them swings the golf club exactly alike. Some PGA Tour players have what is often referred to as a classic swing—Steve Elkington being a prime example. Others compete with extremely unorthodox motions—Jim Furyk's has been compared to falling out of a lawn chair. The differences can be due to physical makeup. Short, stocky players like Craig Stadler and Ian Woosnam usually employ a flatter swing plane. Taller players like Tom Weiskopf and Bob Charles tend to attack the ball from a steeper angle.

Differences can stem from habits developed long ago. Fuzzy Zoeller sets up with the ball planted near the neck of his irons; not many instruction texts will recommend such a position. Bobby Locke employed an extremely shut address position and hit superlative hooks. A lot of top players simply have varying philosophies on the golf swing. Some top touring professionals are extremely meticulous about their golf swings. They approach their mechanics as scientific research. Gary Player, Tom Kite, Nick Faldo, and Colin Montgomerie are all great students of the golf swing. Others, while still paying attention to mechanics, play the game more by feel. Lee Trevino, Seve

Ballesteros, Ben Crenshaw, and Tom Watson are tremendous feel players.

The point is, you don't have to be a disciple of Ben Hogan's *Five Lessons: The Modern Fundamentals of Golf* to enjoy the game, although it is an excellent text. But there are some basics to striking the ball well, and *Golf Skills* will help you master these fundamentals while giving you the confidence to tackle more advanced skills.

The experts debate even some of the basics. Alternative methods to various swing aspects are also available. You will find more detailed explanations of methods for escaping trouble, shaping shots, and getting your ball in the hole once you've reached the green. All of the advice presented is intended to serve as a blueprint for you to develop and refine to your individual style. It is intended to help you get better.

### Building Blocks

Be careful of the temptation to employ some of the more advanced sections of the instruction before mastering the all-important points made regarding grip, stance, and alignment. While these sections are not the most exciting, they are undeniably crucial to continuing along your path to better golf. It requires a fairly advanced understanding of your swing to make adjustments during your stroke. Even with an acute understanding, such adjustments are not recommended. The beginning golfer, however, can make adjustments in grip and setup that will go a long way to improving the overall swing. A mastery of the basics is forever reliable. If things begin to go awry, you can scale back to the basics and hopefully get it right again. If you don't master the basics, you will continue to flail away.

It has been said that the golf swing should be taught as one fluid motion. Thinking of it as such is helpful in developing critical tempo, timing, and balance. But it is actually the combination of and connections between the individual components within the larger motion that allow you to create the flowing stroke. Don't believe for one second that the powerful, seemingly effortless swings of the world's top golfers are not rooted in the very fundamentals mentioned above. No less of an authority than Nick Faldo has admitted he probably tinkers with and refines his grip and setup more than any other aspect of his envied swing. These fundamentals must be mastered before you can hope to get better.

### Do the Time

Chances are that you've played golf with the same flaws for many years. Your body

11

more consistently. It is during this phase where it is most beneficial to work with a professional. He or she can monitor your improvements and give you the encouragement helpful in working through the changes.

It would be wonderful to be able to provide a set of instructions that would transform you into a single-digit handicapper overnight. Unfortunately, that is not possible. Improvement will take time. Rest assured that what you're doing will simplify your swing and make it more dependable.

### Golf School

Not everyone has the patience or inclination to spend a weekly hour one-on-one with their golf professional. Golf, after all, is much more fun to play than to practice. You may prefer to make use of your precious little golf time on the course. This is an understandable point of view. However, your game is not likely to improve at all as you continue to make the same mistakes shot after shot.

An increasingly popular method of gaining crucial instruction is to attend any of the number of golf schools held all over the world. Attendees usually spend mornings in small group instruction with a PGA professional and afternoons on the course. Some offer afternoon rounds with

has ingrained improper motions. Your muscles, joints, and tendons are used to flowing and firing in familiar ways that may or may not be correct. For this reason, integrating new, correct movements into your golf swing will feel very awkward. It will feel wrong. You will be uncomfortable and probably spray shots all over the practice range. Don't get discouraged and do be persistent. Incorporating proper fundamentals into your swing is the only way to develop a repeating, solid stroke that will minimize mistakes and serve you on the course. Eventually the proper movements will become more familiar and you will begin striking the ball

the pro, a unique opportunity to receive practical course management instruction not normally available. There are golf schools that focus exclusively on the short game, golf schools for left-handed players, and golf schools for women only. Individuals are normally grouped into ability levels.

Packages offered at many of the schools include meals, lodging, and playing privileges. You'd have to dig into your vacation time to get to one, some of which last five days or more, but it's a great way to hone your swing and still enjoy your time on the course.

Many of the schools videotape your personal instruction and allow you to take home the footage to study on your own. Some even offer a follow-up video lesson in which you send back your own tape for critique after you've worked on the lessons learned at the camp. This is a unique and valuable tool.

### More than Physical

A positive mental outlook is crucial to becoming a good golfer, especially a golfer with whom people enjoy spending an afternoon! It's often said that you can learn a lot about a person by playing a round of golf with him. If you tend to get

13

frustrated and upset with poor play on the course, not only are you thought of as a boor but also, chances are, your potential to improve your game is severely hampered. It's hard enough to try to make swing adjustments while playing. If you're angry or preoccupied with a particular fault, not only will you be unable to correct it, but the rest of your game will likely suffer as well. It is important to maintain a sense of humor and humility about golf or you'll just continue to get frustrated and lose focus. In addition, the temperamental golfer is seldom invited back out.

### Sources

Thousands of golf instruction texts have been published. The advice contained in *Golf Skills* is espoused by some of the greatest, most consistent swingers of the club: Jack Nicklaus, Tom Kite, Steve Elkington, Nick Price, Nick Faldo, and Tiger Woods are just a few. While these men have many differences in their overall swings, all perform many of the fundamentals in the same way. No one expects you to swing the club exactly like these great champions, but if you can work with their basic ideas, you can develop a solid stroke of your own.

# MASTERING THE BASICS

## Starting Out

Whether you're a beginner just starting out or an experienced golfer, it is important to spend some time working on your game. The question often asked is how much time should be spent practicing and how much time should be spent playing on the course? It depends on exactly what you want out of this wonderful game.

If you have aspirations of becoming a good golfer, then hard work on the practice tee, along with some good instruction, is a must. Spend some time on the range before you tee off, starting with the shorter irons and gradually working up to the woods, focusing mainly on rhythm and balance. If you want to play just for fun, then go out with your friends and don't worry about your score. However, you will still find that some instruction and practice will be helpful.

When you do practice, work on all aspects of the game. Spend 50 percent of your practice time on pitching, chipping, bunker shots, and putting; 25 percent working on your irons; and 25 percent working on your fairway woods and driver.

17

### Practicing at Home

For those of you who have busy lives, hectic careers, and families to take care of, it is not always easy to find time to head to the course or practice range. There are many shots you can practice at home that only take a few minutes a day. The most obvious one is putting. You can work on your putting stroke on your carpet, using a ruler to check your putter head path. You can also practice chipping to a small target, such as a coin or tee, in the yard.

One of the most beneficial things to practice at home is swinging a club, focusing on technique (as seen in 1 to 12). Practice keeps golfing muscles limber, so when you go to the golf course on the weekend, your body will be comfortable with your swing and you will be able to improve fairly quickly. Every beginner should practice regularly for steady improvement.

Ask at your club or the course that you play about who has a good reputation as an instructor in your area. Depending on your goals, set up a series of lessons or go to a golf school to get a solid foundation.

Reading books and magazines on golf can be beneficial. However, the golfer should be selective in deciding which tips to incorporate into his swing, and which tips to stay away from. As the novice golfer can misinterpret the written word on golf tips, consult your teaching pro for clarity and to decide if a given tip will benefit you personally.

10

11

12

# *Grip*

It's been said countless times in golf instruction: Your hands are your only connection to the club. The point is obvious but extremely important and, frankly, overlooked. Your grip determines absolutely everything else that happens in your golf swing. A poor grip eliminates virtually any chance you have of executing a decent stroke. You may not be able to feel where your clubhead is at the top, or the point where your shaft flexes, but you can feel that club in your hands. It is one of those fundamentals that is impossible to overstress. Develop a good grip.

Bad grips are more common than bad swings, and a good player is never seen with a bad grip. The problem begins when the student is unsure which of the three grips is best. It depends on your body type. Do you have strong hands and arms? Are you weak in that area? Are your fingers long and thin or short and pudgy? The answers will determine the right grip for you.

There are three grips taught by golf instructors: the overlapping, or Vardon, grip, the interlocking grip, and the less popular ten-finger, or baseball, grip. Whichever you choose, a good grip is one that's comfortable. It's one that you can repeat consistently. A good grip

allows your hands to work together, not against each other.

Grip pressure is equally as important as how and where you place your hands on the club. Choking the grip adds stress to your entire swing. A tight grip leads to tight forearms, which leads to tight shoulders, and so on. Don't kill your swing before you even take the club away from the ball.

For reasons of clarity, "top hand" and "bottom hand" will be used rather than "left" or "right" for the benefit of left- as well as right-handed golfers.

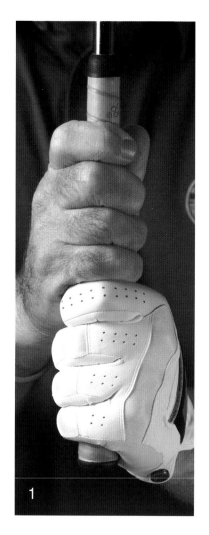

### The Baseball Grip

The baseball, or ten-finger, grip is good for female and senior golfers who do not have a lot of strength in their wrists and forearms. This allows the lower hand to be a little more active through the hitting area, helping rotation to square the clubface, resulting in straighter shots and more distance (1).

### The Overlapping Grip

The overlapping, or Vardon, grip (after Harry Vardon) is the most popular and is suitable for most male and female golfers with strong arms and wrists. It unifies the hands, helping them work as one unit (2).

### The Interlocking Grip

The interlocking grip works well for people with short fingers and pudgy palms who find it difficult to get the small finger to overlap. The small finger of the upper hand and the index finger of the lower hand interlock, unifying the hands and allowing them to work as one unit (3). (Jack Nicklaus uses this grip.) There are a number of common requisites regardless of which grip you choose.

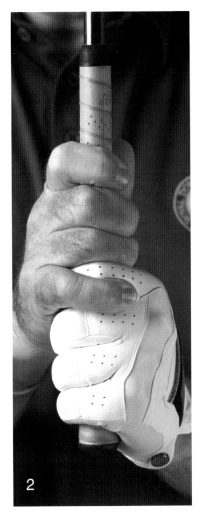

2

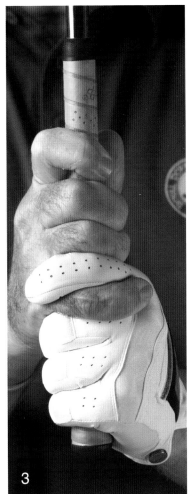

3

### *The Top Hand Position*

The top hand needs to be placed on the club so that looking down at your hands, you can see two knuckles (1 and 2). The line formed by the thumb and the back of the hand must point to the right shoulder (left shoulder for left-handers).

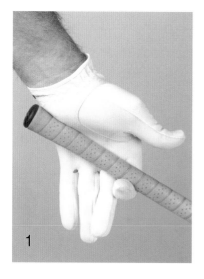

1

2

### The Bottom Hand Position

The bottom hand is placed on the club with the palms adjacent to one another and the lines formed by the thumbs and the back of the hands are parallel to one another. The lifeline of the bottom hand fits snugly over the thumb of the top hand. The thumb and index finger of the bottom hand form a slight "trigger grip" and the tips of each finger touch (3 and 4).

3

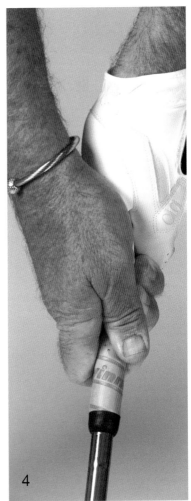

4

### Grip Pressure

You must grip your club firmly enough to maintain control, yet softly enough to avoid unnecessary tension to your hands, arms, and shoulders.

If you can feel your forearms flex, you're holding the club too tight. Try to aim for a neutral grip. A weak grip is the least desirable.

### Grip Strengthening

Plunge your hand right into a bucket of sand and extend then flex your fingers ten times. Repeat with your left hand.

It's important to have strength in your hands because it allows you to control the club more effectively. You're not looking to choke the club, but a firm handle is desirable.

GOLF SKILLS

28

# Stance and Alignment

There are several decisions to be made before you set up to the ball. You must choose the target on which to land your ball, you must choose the right club for the distance to that target, and you must assess the lie you're faced with, among other things. All of these choices affect how you'll eventually set up to the ball.

The physical aspects of setup, stance, and alignment will be explained later, but the overriding theme is comfort. A stable, balanced, and comfortable position will allow you to strike the ball solidly and consistently. A well-struck ball accomplished from an improper setup position is a stroke of luck. Address is where you establish the base on which the rest of the swing depends. If your address position is not dependable, your swing will be unstable.

Setup, stance, and alignment elicit possibly the least amount of controversy from the golf instruction community. Most agree there are few variables in a good address position. It needs to become second nature.

### Aiming the Club

More faults in the golf swing are associated with poor alignment than any other cause. Golfers are often unaware of lining up incorrectly, so problems such as pulling, pushing, and slicing ensue.

Obviously, if you do not line yourself up correctly it is very difficult to hit the ball straight on a consistent basis. Aiming your clubface to the target is critical. Take the scenario of a golfer with a good golf swing who unknowingly aims slightly to the right of his target. He makes a perfect swing and the ball misses his target to the right. He automatically assumes that he has made a poor swing, and when lining up to the next shot, tries to correct the fault by

pulling the ball back on-line. An "over the top" swing now starts to develop, where the clubhead path cuts across the ball, and soon this good golf swing has lost its power and direction. As these problems persist, the golfer continually tries to correct them by correcting a fault with a fault. The first thing that needs to be corrected is alignment. Pay attention to your own alignment and never hit a shot while you are lined up incorrectly.

Whether hitting a drive, iron shot, fairway wood, or a putt, the alignment

LEFT: *Shoulders parallel, stance parallel to ball-to-target line.*

G O L F   S K I L L S

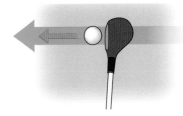

ABOVE: *Ball travels straight.*

procedure is the same. There are two lines associated with aiming: the target line, a line drawn from the ball to the target, and the body line, a line drawn through the toes parallel to the target line. In fact your toes, hips, and shoulders are aiming slightly left of the target in order to have the clubface perfectly aligned to the target.

On the practice tee, always place a club down on the ground to help you with alignment and to prevent poor swing habits from developing because of bad alignment. Golfers can get so wrapped up working on their swing mechanics that they totally forget about alignment. Never start a practice session without a specific target, particularly when working on your full swing. By always using a club for alignment during a practice session, you get used to lining up correctly, and this will carry over to the golf course. You can also incorporate alignment into your preshot routine.

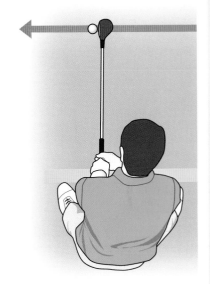

ABOVE: *Stance and shoulders parallel.*

BELOW: *Correct lie of the club. There should be a small gap between the toe of the club and the ground.*

31

### Stance

Your stance should be about as wide as your shoulders for all clubs when you are using a full swing. As there is only one golf swing for all standard full shots, use the same width stance regardless of whether you are hitting a driver or an iron.

The back foot should be set at ninety degrees to the target line, and the front foot turned out about thirty degrees. Squaring off the back foot creates a stable back leg and prevents swaying. By toeing the front foot out slightly, you are able to clear your body easier on the downswing.

The only time you should widen your stance is on a windy day, to prevent the

1

wind from blowing you off balance. Your weight should be distributed evenly between the heels and toes of both feet, with the weight slightly on the inside of both feet at the address position.

### Square Stance

A square stance occurs when both feet are positioned along the body line and square to the target line (1). The knees, hips, and shoulders should also be square to this line. This stance should be used most of the time.

### Open Stance

An open stance has the front foot pulled slightly back from the body line (2). This stance allows the hips to clear quicker on the downswing and will promote a slight outside-in swing, which will, in turn, produce a fade. The knees, hips, and shoulders are pointing slightly left of the target line.

### Closed Stance

A closed stance occurs when the back foot is pulled slightly back from the body line (3). This stance allows the hips to rotate a little more in the backswing and promotes a slightly bigger shoulder turn. It also helps to produce a draw. The knees, hips, and shoulders are pointing slightly right of the target line.

2

3

### Spine Tilt/Knee Flex

Approach your ball and focus on your target from behind. Don't get over your ball and then look to see if you're aligned properly. Relax, with your knees slightly bent and your arms hanging straight down from your shoulders. Many amateurs set up to the ball in a close fashion because they're sure they're going to slice it. A closed stance will increase the chances of slicing. Always remember to bend from your waist.

### Rotation/Balance

Your stance should be solid enough that a person would be unable to push you over from the front or back. Your spine angle must remain constant. If it moves throughout your swing you are actually changing your distance from the ball. It's nearly impossible to return your clubface squarely to the ball if you've altered your distance from it.

BELOW: *Spine angle should remain constant.*

35

### The Address Position

For reasons of clarity for both left- and right-handed golfers, the terms "front" and "back," rather than "left" or "right" are used here. For example, the front foot would be the left foot for right-handers.

### Setup: Width of Stance

The stance should be approximately the width of the shoulders for the middle irons (1), slightly narrower for the shorter clubs, and slightly wider for the longer clubs (with emphasis on the word "slightly"). The back foot should be set at ninety degrees to your target line in order to prevent the hip from sliding laterally on the backswing. The front foot should be turned out slightly in order to facilitate the clearing of the front side on the downswing.

### Hand Position

This is an often neglected position at address. It is important that there is a straight line from the top of the front shoulder to the ball (2). This sets the hands in the correct position relative to the ball position. Note that the butt of the club should be over the middle of the front thigh regardless of which club is in your hand.

1

2

### Posture

Only slightly bend your knees (too much bend causes all sorts of problems with the backswing). Your arms should hang down vertically from the shoulders. This helps keep any tension out of the arms at the address position. Tension in the arms at address also causes problems on the backswing. The spine should be relatively straight and the chin held slightly away from the chest.

### Address Positions

Your forearms should be even. Your clubhead's leading edge should be square to your target line. This position gives you the best chance to hit the ball consistently.

Try to set your clubhead behind the ball before you step into the stance to ensure it's pointed at your target.

### Waggle and Relaxation

There needs to be a certain amount of motion over the ball. Too many amateurs are static at address.

Many golfers wiggle their feet or waggle the club to release tension. Check your intended line of flight to ensure proper alignment.

### Ball Position:

### The Irons

The ball position for all regular iron shots (not low/high/uphill/downhill lies) is about two inches inside the front heel. This automatically sets the hands slightly ahead of the ball and helps give the desired "slightly downward" blow that is required for crisp iron shots (1).

BELOW: *Straight-shot waggle.*

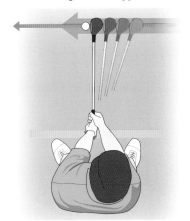

1

### The Fairway Woods

The ball position for the fairway woods is directly off the left heel. This automatically sets the hands even with the ball and helps give the desired "bottom of the arc" blow required for lofted fairway shots (2).

### The Drive

The ball position for the driver is off the instep of the front foot. This sets the hands even with the clubhead and helps give the desired "slightly upward" blow required for good tee shots (3).

2

3

BELOW: *Where to place the ball.*

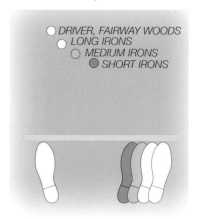

*DRIVER, FAIRWAY WOODS*
*LONG IRONS*
*MEDIUM IRONS*
*SHORT IRONS*

# Takeaway

You may think it unnecessary to devote an entire section to the takeaway, but the swing's first several inches are from where the rest of your backswing grows. Mess up this part of your stroke and the only way you'll get the club back on line is to manipulate it in some unnatural way. This is a growth pattern for disaster.

The takeaway provides one of the most frequently used swing maxims: "low and slow." The fact that it is rooted in the takeaway suggests just how important this part of your swing should be. Not only do you set the pattern for your backswing here, you also, if done correctly, establish the tempo for the remainder of your swing.

Just where the preswing ends and the takeaway begins is a matter of debate. Golfers initiate their swing with differing amounts of motion. But the takeaway should not be started from a static position. The golf swing is an athletic motion. A certain amount of movement is expected prior to taking the club back. If you don't move about or wiggle your feet slightly, you're certain to possess too much tension.

### Takeaway Technique

The first few inches you take the club back should be directly along your target line. The movement is made with your arms, shoulders, and hands as one piece. Don't let the clubhead get behind you too quickly.

### Takeaway Drill

Practice on the range with two clubs in "railroad track" formation behind your ball.

Many golfers tend to yank the club inside immediately on the backswing. The takeaway is a motion made primarily with your shoulders, so avoid manipulating the club back with your hands.

RIGHT: *To obtain the correct alignment to the target, imagine a railroad track.*

### Preshot Routine

The next time you watch golf on TV, notice what the players do before they play each shot. Each one of them goes through a preshot routine, which will be exactly the same each time. Many students of golf say that they would like to be more consistent and this is one way to ensure that. Each pro has his or her own preshot routine and you will probably want to develop your own.

Two elements that should be included in the routine are visualization and alignment.

The routine you perform before starting the clubhead back is important for you both mentally and physically. A good preshot routine, as executed in the next two pages, allows you to aim properly, relax your mind, and set up to your ball with the best chance of hitting a solid shot.

There are countless ways to prepare to hit your ball. The important thing about a preshot routine is that you develop one and follow it to the letter every time. You can have a simple, quick routine or a complicated, drawn-out saga of a

routine. Often a golfer's preshot routine corresponds to his overall mental outlook. A feel-type golfer tends to get through the set quickly. The more thoughtful golfer may labor through the choreography.

A preshot routine begins from behind the ball. This is the only place you have the opportunity to view your target and line of flight with an undistorted eye. That's why the preshot routine is so important to aim and alignment. The greatest asset of a well-rehearsed preshot routine is the opportunity it provides for you to settle down, calm your nerves, and take a deep breath. It is here you eliminate all fears and develop confidence.

Take your first practice swing next to the ball (1). (Some players prefer to take their practice swing behind the ball, which is fine as well.)

Stand behind the ball and visualize the flight of the shot you are about to hit. It will help program your subconscious into producing the exact shot required (2).

Once that is done, pick a spot about two feet in front of your ball but in line with your target. Walk around and align the clubface to that spot (3). It is much easier to line up to something close to you rather than a long way off, so pick an intermediate target. Go into the address position and hit your shot (4).

A preshot routine will not only help with consistency but the visualization will improve your overall game. The key point to remember is: Do the same thing each time and don't vary your routine, in order to maintain consistency.

# THE SWING

ABOVE: *Backswing*

ABOVE: *Downswing*

ABOVE: *Follow-through*

One question which is asked more than any other is: Once I'm in my address position, what is the correct way to start the swing? The answer is more complex than the question suggests.

Much has been written about the takeaway, such as take it back with the left side or the right side, or use the arms to take it back using your muscles or hands. There isn't any particular way to take the club back in terms of how it feels, only in terms of where the club should be at particular times during the swing. Although we may all have the same bone and muscle structure, we have different perceptions on how things feel. The only instruction that can be given is to indicate where the club should be at each point on the swing. When the student is in the correct position, only he or she knows how it feels for them and how best to achieve it.

# Backswing

The backswing is perhaps the most important part of your golf swing. This is where you generate your power and begin the crucial transition to the downswing. The backswing is where your weight begins to shift, your wrists break, and you start to turn around your body. This is where the golf swing truly becomes an athletic movement. This is where coordination takes over. Not surprisingly, this is also where the better golfers start to distinguish themselves from the hackers.

BELOW: *The start of the backswing.*

Backswing technique varies from golfer to golfer. Mostly this depends on physical makeup. You may get the club back flatter or steeper depending on your size and range of motion. The important thing is to establish a plane for the remainder of your swing and to stick with it. It is dangerous to think of manipulating the club onto a specific plane. Your backswing should feel natural, not contrived. The only way you'll be able to get the club moving back toward the ball with any consistency is if you take it back similarly.

You're fighting gravity on the way back and the sensation is strange. But remember, you're really only storing it.

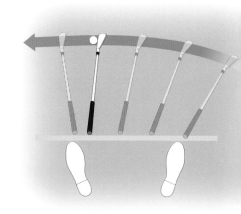

### Backswing Technique

The target line and body line has been mentioned in relation to the address position. At the start of the takeaway, you want the hands to move straight back along the body line with no manipulation or rotation of the hands or arms. In other words, the hands are passive and the torso rotates.

Halfway up the backswing, the club position should appear as in 1 and 2. As you can see, the clubhead is still slightly

1

2

3

outside the body line. It is important not to confuse this statement to mean the clubhead is outside the target line. If the club moved straight back, the arms would pull away from the body. Most good players today have the club in this position, including Nicklaus, Couples, and Els, among others.

What you do not want is for the club to get behind you or to get too much on the inside, as this causes the wrists to rotate, laying the clubface open. This ultimately lays the club off (pointing to the left for right-handed golfers) at the top of the backswing, a sure way of starting the downswing "over the top."

If the grip pressure is light at this point the wrists will start to "cock" naturally with the momentum of the clubhead and the club will start to break upward. At this stage the hands are approximately in the middle of the chest and the club will feel very light in your hands (3 and 4).

Continue with a full shoulder turn to the top of the backswing (5 and 6).

4

5

6

As the club continues back, your wrists begin to hinge and your upper body should rotate against the slight turn of your hips. Don't be afraid to let your wrists cock fully. Your arms and body work together as a unit.

Be careful not to take the club too far back. When you go too far back, you're out of balance and you have to make adjustments to get back to the ball.

At the top, nearly all of your weight should be on your back leg in an athletic and comfortably positioned coil. Allow your shoulders to turn fully, but only take the club back to where you think it's three-quarters full. This should put you exactly where you need to be.

## Other Points to Note on the Backswing

The right knee does not move from its original position, all the way to the top of the swing. This stable position ensures that the proper torque is created in the body.

The left arm stays reasonably straight, not rigid, throughout the backswing, especially at the top of the swing, a definite problem area for a lot of golfers. If the left arm breaks down, you will again lose that torque that produces the necessary power on the downswing.

The weight moves over to the right side at the top of the backswing, with the sternum directly over the right foot. This prevents a "reverse pivot," ensuring the proper weight shift and making the start of the downswing a lot easier and more powerful.

1

### Swing Plane
There are two swing planes to be aware of: the shaft plane and the arm plane.

### The Shaft Plane
Halfway up the backswing, the shaft should be either pointing at the ball or slightly inside the ball (1). You definitely do not want the shaft pointing outside the ball line (2). This is called "laying the club off."

### The Arm Plane
The arm plane is a line drawn at address from the ball through the shoulders and extending upward. At the top of the backswing, the left arm should be on the line shown in 3.

Making both of these moves will ensure you are swinging the club "on plane." Practice these moves in front of a mirror in order to both see and feel the correct positions, so that when you go to the practice tee, you'll know what to strive for.

2

3

# Downswing

The downswing, also called the forward swing, is your opportunity to let gravity work for you. It's important to think in terms of unwinding and riding gravity because this helps prevent you from yanking the club from the top. The downswing begins as your club ceases to go backward and starts to come forward toward the ball—also known as the transition. The transition is the point where your club is the farthest away from you and thus feels the least controllable. It's not a comfortable position but also not one to be feared. You must be confident that through your setup, your takeaway, and your backswing, you've given yourself every opportunity to return the clubhead back to the ball with the proper motion. If you've done everything correctly up to this point, the rest should be easy. Of course, it's not.

Earlier it was stated that many feel the golf swing should be taught as one fluid motion. Nowhere is this truer than in the downswing. Focusing on the return of the clubhead back to the ball can produce some scary results. If you allow it to happen naturally, while being aware of the proper mechanics, you'll have the most success.

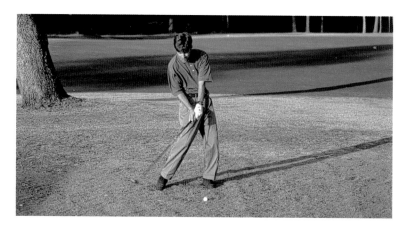

### Downswing Technique

Starting from the top of the backswing, the first move of the downswing starts with the left side (for right-handed golfers). It does not start with the arms, as is so commonly seen among high and medium handicap golfers.

Note that the weight has started to shift across to the front side and the angle created by the shaft and the left arm has not changed. This indicates that the downswing has not been started with the hands.

Any attempt to start the downswing with the hands and arms will immediately cause two things to happen. One, you will "come over the top" and two, you will

1

2

3

instantly lose that all-important shaft angle and get what is called "casting" because it is like casting a fishing rod. This means instant power loss and directional loss as well. In picture 2 (on previous page) the hands have already passed hip level and the angle created by the shaft and left arm is still the same as it was at the top of the backswing. The weight is now approximately 60 percent across onto the front side.

The all important "impact" position is shown in picture 3 (see previous page). If you compare 2 with 3, you can see that the hands have moved approximately a foot in the same time that the clubhead has moved five feet, obviously creating tremendous clubhead speed. At impact your weight should be approximately 70 percent over to the front side and the left arm and shaft are in a straight line. At this moment all the power that has been stored up during the downswing is being released at the correct point, at impact.

Any golfer wanting to improve his or her distance has only to look to these areas to see where the power is being lost. A lesson with the use of a video camera will quickly illustrate this. Once you understand the principles involved in creating "the power move," you will be pleased to see your distance increase and your score come down.

### Incorrect Position of the Forearm

Fault: Most golfers allow the right forearm to get out of "perpendicular" too soon on the downswing. This causes the hands to get too far away from the body, which in turn will cause you to cut across the ball, causing a slice or a pull, depending on where the clubface is at impact.

Cure: From the top of the backswing (1), drop the right arm down so that the forearm is still pointing directly behind you halfway down the downswing (2). The hands should stay close to the body until just before impact. This will produce an inside-out clubhead path, allowing the clubhead to travel down the line toward the target (3).

# The Follow-Through

Why worry about the follow-through? The ball is gone and it will not make any difference. However, a good follow-through can help you get better scores.

You can learn a lot by being aware of your position at the end of your swing. Watch the touring pros after they hit a shot during competition. They hold their follow-through position as they watch the flight of the ball. Their balance is good and all of their weight is on their front leg.

2

1

In fact they can lift the back foot and still keep their balance.

All the weight in picture 1 is on the front foot and the arms have completed their momentum over the shoulder. The back foot is right up on the toe and the sole of the back shoe (2) is visible. This is the ideal position for the follow-through.

The follow-through is mainly the result of what has gone before. In other words, the backswing is the setup of the swing, the downswing is creating the power, and the follow-through will indicate what transpired during those phases. During your practice sessions, hold your position at the end of the swing and try to feel where you are.

If you don't complete your follow-through, you will restrict the speed of the clubhead through the ball. Don't make this mistake. A complete swing includes a full, balanced finish.

A less-than-complete finish will not only sap power from your stroke, it usually causes you to pull your head, and thus your body, which greatly reduces your chance of hitting the ball squarely. This is another power sapper and normally will

cause the ball to be hit off-line. An incomplete follow-through is also an indication that there exists an element of tension during the whole swing. In addition, not following through is often a result of poor balance.

Following are some of the things to look for and how to correct them:

• Is all your weight on the front foot or do you still have some weight on the back? If so, work on improving your weight shift by starting the downswing with a lateral slide of the hips, moving the weight from your back foot (3) to your front foot (4) before the clubhead gets to the ball. If

3

4

movement of the hips, allowing you to keep the clubhead in line to your target (6), which will allow you to finish in a balanced position with your hands above and over your shoulder (7).

• Are your hands finishing just in front of your body (8) instead of following right through (7)? This is an indication of not clearing the left hip fast enough as you swing through the ball. This will almost certainly cause a lack of power or loss in distance. Most students who finish in this position are those who like to play a lot but do not put in the necessary time on

**5**

you have done this correctly, there will be no weight on your back foot at the end of your swing.

• Are your hands finishing low across the front of your body as in picture 5? This is usually caused by spinning the hips right from the top of your backswing, causing the clubhead to cut across the ball and your hands to finish below the shoulder. Start the downswing by transferring your weight to your front foot with a lateral

**6**

the practice tee. They start steering the ball in order to keep the ball in play. To fully trust your swing on the course, you must put the time in on the practice range, making positive, aggressive swings.

• If you are losing your balance forward, as in 9 (see following page), you are probably starting the downswing with your upper body instead of your legs. Again, weight shift, a good extension of the arms down the target line, and a complete body rotation is important, allowing the

7

8

weight to move to the left heel with the belt buckle ending up facing the target (7).

In order to play good, consistent golf, you have to put some time in on the practice range. This is where you can develop a sound, repetitive swing. You can't do this on a course. Remember to pay close attention to your follow-through in the future—it is more important than you think.

## *Posture*

Incorrect posture will create many problems during both the backswing and the downswing. Spine angle is critical to hitting good golf shots, and if set in the wrong position at address, cannot be corrected during the swing.

Fault: Poor posture at address, with the spine curved, the shoulders slumped.

9

**1**

Poor posture at address, with knees stiff and arms extended outward.

Cure: Take a club and put it behind your back, with the shaft touching both your head and the base of your spine (1). Lean forward slightly from the waist, keeping the shaft in contact with your head and the base of your spine (2). Remove the club, maintain this position, and place the club on the ground. This is the correct spine angle at address, and it will allow you to make a proper turn on the backswing. The knees are slightly flexed and the arms hang comfortably.

**2**

# Drills for More Distance

We all seek more distance and manufacturers use this desire to sell us new equipment each year. However, good swing mechanics will help you develop more power than any new driver.

### The Baseball Drill

Take your driver, and holding it out in front of you, make a turn horizontally as if you were swinging a baseball bat (1). Now swing through as hard as you can, trying to make the "whoosh" sound happen beyond the front of your body (2). In other words, the whoosh happens beyond where you started the club. In order to do this correctly, you have to use your body and not your arms. Once you have this feeling of creating power with your torso, go back to your regular stance and try to duplicate the same feeling. You'll hear the whoosh after impact, telling you that you have reached maximum clubhead speed at impact, resulting in more distance.

**1**

**2**

3

### *The Whoosh Drill*

If you have a problem creating the whoosh described in the previous drill, flip the club over and hold the club by the head (3). Again swing the club, trying to create the whoosh after the impact position (4). You will discover that you can only do this if you turn the body ahead of the arms. Re-create this feeling with the club the right way around and you will start seeing your drives fly farther!

4

### Increasing the Width of Your Arc Drill

The bigger your arc on the backswing, the more clubhead speed you will produce on the downswing. However, most golfers think they are creating a wide arc when in fact they are not. Test yourself in the following manner to see if you are taking the club back as wide as you can.

Put your head cover behind the head of your driver (5) and as you start your backswing (6), push the head cover straight back. If you can push the head cover beyond your right foot, you are taking the club back correctly. If not, you are picking your club up too quickly with your hands (7).

5

6

7

# Timing, Tempo, Rhythm

Golf is an athletic movement. The swing requires strength, flexibility, and a certain amount of grace. It's not enough to master the mechanics of grip, setup, backswing, and downswing, etc. You must be able to meld all of these steps into a well-choreographed movement. This is done with timing, tempo, and balance. A mechanically sound golfer without these elements in his stroke is not difficult to spot. He's the robotic-looking fellow.

To develop a sound swing, it is necessary to break it down into its basic parts. Then, as suggested, you must master these parts before you can hope to put them all together. But in all the practice and drills you employ, you must always maintain a sense of timing, tempo, and rhythm.

A good golf swing resembles a ballet movement. Good golfers make their strokes look effortless. They do this with superior tempo and rhythm.

The biggest problem many golfers have is trying to hit the ball too hard. This usually means they take the club back too far and then try to kill it. It's important to have good timing in this situation.

Take the same amount of time in your backswing as you do in the forward swing. This notion also helps you build consistency.

BELOW: *Don't hit the ball—swing rhythmically through it.*

# WOOD PLAY

The importance placed on long drives is comical. The galleries assembled for Tour big hitters John Daly, Tiger Woods, and Davis Love III, among others, are massive because everyone likes to see these guys launch their tee shots. And it is indeed impressive to watch the ball fly far down the fairway and tumble 300 yards away. But you'll notice that these players are not achieving their distance by trying to hit their drives hard (well, maybe Daly). Their distance is achieved by swinging smoothly, with excellent tempo and precise balance.

Amateur golfers are too preoccupied with distance at the expense of accuracy. The driver is a difficult club to hit. The shaft is long, there is less loft on the face, and your swing is bigger. All of these elements combine to reduce your chances of striking the ball properly. When your mental state is to kill the ball to achieve maximum distance, you're sure to decrease the odds even further. Once you've made the decision to use a driver off the tee—and this should not be an automatic decision—realize this should be the most calmly swung club in your bag.

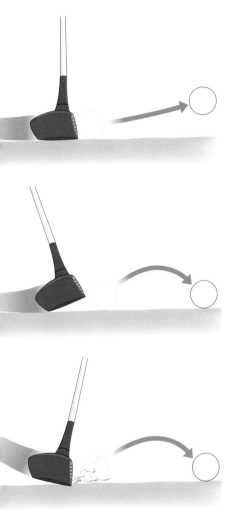

### Fairway Woods

Golfers have trouble with fairway woods because they incorrectly judge the shot. Some treat the shot the same way as they would their driver. Because it is a wood, they think that they should swing it in the same way.

Some try to lift the ball off the ground, either collapsing their left arm (for right-handed golfers) or straightening up in an effort to get the ball airborne. Both efforts result in either a topped shot, or hitting a ball without much height off the bottom of the club.

ABOVE: *Perfect strike*

CENTER: *Topped shot*

BELOW: *Bad shot*

### Ball Position

This is often the main culprit of poor fairway wood shots. Most golfers err in positioning the ball the same as with their driver. They place it off the instep of the front foot.

In the address position with a fairway wood, the ball position is directly opposite the left heel. With a normal golf swing, this represents the bottom of the arc, which is exactly where to make contact with the ball.

Go ahead and swing, making sure you get the feeling of driving the ball forward and not up. This is accomplished by keeping the clubhead low and long through the hitting area (1). Make an aggressive swing through the ball, and try not to "steer" the ball down the fairway (2). Let the follow-through go right over your left shoulder.

If your fairway woods are a problem on the golf course, don't avoid them on the practice range. Work on the correct technique to gain the confidence to hit the shots well. Once you start hitting your fairway woods well on the practice range, you will have no problem carrying that swing over to the golf course.

### How to Swing at 90 Percent

Most amateurs know that 105 percent feeling, but here is a way to develop that famous Ernie Els or Freddie Couples "syrupy" swing.

Warm up at the range first. Then start hitting an 8-iron at your "flat out" 100 percent swing and mark down the yardage. Using an 8-iron as an example, you may hit 160 yards at 100 percent. Now divide that by two, and start hitting that same 8-iron to your new yardage. This now becomes your 50 percent swing, in this example 80 yards. It is important to practice this swing in order to teach yourself the control you will need later. Now set a new target at 75 percent

of your distance, in this example 120 yards, and practice hitting this shot consistently to that target. This is now your 75 percent swing. See how easy it feels.

Finally, 90 percent of 160 yards is 144 yards and this is the swing to use on the course. It is aggressive to hit the 8-iron 160 yards, but your ball striking and accuracy will improve vastly without having to change anything major in your swing.

One of the other benefits of this 90 percent swing is that if you are between clubs, you can always go down one club and swing a little harder to get the desired distance. This gives you many more options on the course.

In pictures 1, 2, and 3 (p. 73), the takeaway is long, slow, and deliberate. In pictures 4, 5, and 6 (p. 74), the momentum of the club works upward, the sign of good technique and a soft grip pressure. In pictures 7 and 8 (p. 75), the torso makes a complete turn and the left shoulder is under the chin. The weight has shifted to the front foot at the start of the downswing (9 and 10) and the club is "lagging," indicating that no attempt is made to hit with the arms. Picture 12 shows the end result of doing everything correctly. The club is working directly down the line to the target, ensuring a straight shot.

### Woods Versus Irons?

A frequently asked question is: How do I adjust my swing for woods versus irons?

First of all, you do not want to adjust your swing or swing your woods differently from your irons. The swings are basically the same. The only difference is that the plane of the swing will be a little "flatter" with the woods than the irons due to the longer shaft.

The plane of the swing is a line drawn from the ball through the shoulders and extending on up. At the top of the backswing, the back of the left hand (for right-handed golfers) should be on this line.

Most golfers will hit a 5-wood better than a 3-wood and a 3-wood better than a driver because of the loft of the club. A 5-wood will have more backspin and less sidespin than a 3-wood, and the same will apply with the 3 versus the driver. With the driver, there is minimum backspin and even a slight error in clubface angle or clubhead path will result in sidespin, and the greater the clubhead speed the more off-line the ball will travel. Even the touring pros will tend to tee off with a 3-wood when accuracy is more important than distance. Just watch the U.S. Open, where the rough is traditionally punishing—the pros will be teeing off with 3-woods and 2-irons quite often.

BELOW: *Wood and iron swing planes.*

*SWING PLANE OF WOOD*
*SWING PLANE OF IRON*

# IRON PLAY

Most golfers feel reasonably comfortable operating with their short and middle irons—the 9-iron through 5-iron. The shafts are shorter than the long irons and woods, so you are able to stand closer to the ball. You are less inclined to "help" the ball into the air because you trust the higher lofts built into the short and middle irons.

Your accuracy with the short and middle irons allows you to get the ball nearer the hole and to produce lower scores. Therefore, it is important to know what distances you can obtain from each of these clubs. Spend some time on a well-marked practice range—even this method is difficult—and gauge how far each of your irons flies. Normally, you should expect about a ten yard distance gap between each one.

Once on course, be careful to gauge accurately the distance to the hole. Once you're comfortable you've got the right distance and have selected the right club, swing with confidence. You know you can hit it.

### Long Irons

The long irons are played with the ball slightly back in your stance. You don't have to hit long irons hard. Let the club do the work. Don't be intimidated by the decreased loft. Strike the ball first and swing smoothly.

No matter what iron you're using, it's important to focus on making a full shoulder turn. This helps you maximize your distance potential and increases the likelihood you will finish with full follow-through.

### Fade

Set the clubface directly on the line you want the ball to start. Open your stance relative to that line and swing along your shoulders.

Many people will hit this shot too hard and end up double-crossing themselves. Instead of cutting the ball, the face remains closed and you pull it.

The ball will start along the line and your outside-to-in swing path will cause the ball to move from left to right. Focus on the area where you want the ball to start turning. Obviously, you want the ball to turn to the pin, but you want to focus on the target where it's going to turn.

### Draw

Set the clubface directly on the line you want the ball to start. Close your stance relative to that line and swing along your shoulders.

Focus on taking the club away on a definite inside path. This is the best method to get the club to come back from the inside, resulting in the right-to-left ball flight.

The ball will start along the line and your inside-to-out swing path will cause the ball to move from right to left.

Another technique for drawing the ball is to align your feet on the line you want the ball to start and point your clubface at the target.

### Creating Spin

Play the ball slightly forward and choke down on the grip. You must strike the ball first and accelerate through impact.

Concentrate on hitting the ball. This will help ensure that you contact the ball on the way down and don't catch it thin by pulling up through the ball. Don't take too steep an angle to the ball.

You must strike the ball first and accelerate through impact.

# PITCHING

The difficulty of pitching should not be underestimated. Pitching is tough, as there are so many variables to consider. For example, do you want to hit a pitch shot that stops immediately next to the hole? The answer is only if you must.

In any case, few high-handicap players can put the right amount of backspin on the ball to stop it dead on landing. Do you want to pitch the ball halfway to the hole and let it run close? Only if you can. Pitching is an exercise in decision making and then mechanics.

Pitching is also difficult because so many pitch shots are less than full swings. Any time you must manipulate the length of your swing, you increase the chance of doing something wrong. You'll get the mechanics of pitching later. For now, focus on your decision making.

The basic idea is that you want to keep your ball as close to the ground as possible. It's much easier to determine what your ball will do if it's rolling. The axiom has always been: If you can't putt it, chip it. If you can't chip it, run it to the hole. If you can't run it, then, and only then, fly it to the hole. It's always romantic to consider yourself a wedge wizard, but the smart player only lofts the ball when it's necessary.

Most amateurs hit the ball well from tee to green, but it is when they get within 50 yards of the green that they seem to struggle. "I don't have time to practice these shots," they say. "The pros have all the time in the world to stand and work on these shots, so they develop feel."

Here is a method that requires a little practice initially, but once you have established your distances, you will be able to rely on it in the future.

### The Technique

The ball position is approximately two inches inside the left heel. The stance is slightly open, presetting the left hip in an open position, which will allow you to clear the left side later on in the downswing. Most of the weight is set forward on the left foot, which will push the hands slightly forward, setting the shaft ahead of the ball. This allows for a slightly downward blow, to create the height and backspin you need for this shot. The feet are fairly close together, allowing for an easier body rotation. If the feet are too wide apart, you will have trouble turning quickly enough through this shot.

### Pitching Swing

The absolute key to solid pitching is rhythm. No matter if you're attempting a half, three-quarter, or full pitch shot, concentrate on swinging with equal tempo. Control the entire shot with your body and not just your arms.

### The 7-8-9-10 Distance Method

Imagine as you address the ball that you have a large clock in front of you. Learn to swing your left arm (right arm for left-handers) to the various "hours" of the clock.

In the 7 o'clock position (1), there is a slight wrist cock. This is important as you need to cock the wrist to help deliver a slightly downward blow through the shot. Practice hitting balls like this until you can consistently hit shots a certain distance. This will become your 7 o'clock shot.

In the 8 o'clock position (2), practice hitting balls in the same manner, swinging your left arm to 8 o'clock, and note your distances. This will become your

8 o'clock shot. In the 9 o'clock position (3), practice the same technique as with the first two shots, while swinging your left arm to 9 o'clock. Finish off swinging the left arm to 10 o'clock (4) and you will now have four specific distances that you can consistently pitch the ball.

Distances will vary from player to player as in full shots, but once you have them established, you have a tried and true method to rely on. When you find yourself 40 yards from the flag on the course you can say to yourself, "OK, this is my 9 o'clock shot," for example, and you know for sure that if you swing your arm to that position, the ball is going to go about 40 yards.

1

2

3

4

### Key Features of Pitching

At address the majority of your weight should be on your front foot (1). This keeps your body steady during the swing and helps you impart the downward blow important in creating the backspin you want on this shot. Note also, looking at the other positions during the backswing, that your weight does not shift to the back foot at any time. Keep your weight on the front foot even at the top of the backswing. This is only for the pitch shot—not for full shots.

It is important that the pace of the swing be consistent throughout. The pace is controlled by starting the downswing with a rotation of the torso and not with your arms. Any attempt to speed up through the hitting area will definitely cause inconsistent results. It is no good swinging slowly through one shot and quickly through the next. Try to imagine a pendulum and the way it moves backward and forward at the same pace. Try to follow this pace in all of your pitch shots.

The left arm stays straight throughout this entire shot from the address position (1), your backswing (2 and 3), impact position, and follow-through (4 and 5). A bent left arm will result in inconsistent direction and you'll also have a tendency to hit the ball thin (or blade the ball). Lastly, as you see here, it is important to follow

**3**

**4**

through. Do not stop your follow-through on this shot or you will constantly come up short. The follow-through should finish at about 3 o'clock (4 and 5).

Finally, be sure to follow through directly at the target and not around your body. The hands should finish in about the middle of your chest (5).

With just a little practice to establish your distances and pace, you will find playing these shots a lot more fun. You'll also get a lot of comments from your playing partners such as "Where did you learn to pitch all of a sudden?"

**5**

### The Lob Shot

The difference between the pitch shot and a lob shot is that the lob shot is a much shorter, softer-landing shot and will usually be played inside of 30 yards. Vital to the lob shot is the right equipment. You need a 60-degree wedge or a sand wedge with very little bounce.

To play this shot correctly you have to open the clubface, and if you use a sand wedge with a high degree of "bounce" (picture 1), the flange will strike the ground first, causing the leading edge to hit the ball and resulting in a sculled shot

With a 60-degree wedge, you can open the clubface and still slide the clubhead under the ball (picture 2).

**1**

**2**

### Technique

Take a fairly long backswing while fully cocking the wrists (1). Control the downswing with the torso and not the arms, maintaining the wrist cock and keeping the blade open throughout the shot (2). Finally, the follow-through will end with the clubface still facing the sky (3).

The real secret of this shot is to not allow the fingers to pass the pad of the right hand. This shot takes a lot of practice in order to master the technique needed for success on the course. However, the results will have a positive effect on your score and you'll feel great satisfaction in having mastered this beautiful shot.

### Punch Low/Spinner

Play the ball back in your stance and make just a three-quarter swing. Think of trapping the ball and restrict your follow-through.

Get the ball on the ground as soon as you can. Then it can follow like a putt. The more you try to fly the ball to the flag, the more likely you are to make an error.

## *Flop Shot*

This shot is useful when you must carry the ball to the hole and land it softly. Play the ball back in your stance and choke down.

Lay your clubface wide open. Think of swishing the clubhead right under your ball. Concentrate on rhythm and commit to the shot. The harder you hit this shot, the higher the ball is going to go.

### Soft and Lofted (Left)

A high-lofted pitch from the fairway is one of golf's most difficult situations. Open your body and the clubface and try to clip the ball off the turf.

Concentrate on hitting the back of the ball first. Don't take a lot of turf with it. You want to just pick it off the turf.

### Low Spinner (Right)

This miniature punch shot allows you to top your ball quickly. Close down your clubface and smother the ball into the turf.

If you must fly it, focus on the green where you want to land the ball. Too many golfers just focus on the pin.

# Wedge Mania

There has been a lot of hype in the last few years over pitching, sand, and lob wedges, but high handicap golfers do not have the skill to warrant more than three wedges, and the lower handicap golfer has enough skill to only need three wedges.

### The Pitching Wedge

Usually about 50 degrees in loft, this club is sometimes called a 10-iron, and should be used for full shots into the green (anywhere from 60 to 120 yards depending on your handicap) and chipping (1).

**1**

### The Sand Wedge

Usually about 55 degrees, this club should not be restricted to the sand only. This very versatile club can be used from 50 to 110 yards with a full swing, sand play around the green, or chipping. Be careful on hardpan or fairly firm bunkers as the sand wedge has "bounce" as seen in the picture, causing the back edge of the flange to hit the ground first. This means that the leading edge of the club would not get under the ball and you would scull the shot (2).

**2**

**3**

### The Lob Wedge

Usually about 60 degrees, this is the most versatile club in the bag and can be used for pitching, sand play (out of firm sand), and chipping. This club has very little or no bounce and can therefore get under the ball, even on hardpan or very tight lies on the fairway (3).

### Recommended Clubs

Try to carry a 50-degree pitching wedge, a 55-degree sand wedge, and a 60-degree lob wedge. This provides an equal gap between the three clubs, which gives equal yardage not only with full shots, but will allow you to control your distance pretty accurately with your pitch shots. This also eliminates the "gap" wedge sold with many sets, allowing you to carry an additional club for longer shots.

### Example Scale of Pitch Shots:

- 30 yards: 7 o'clock shot—lob wedge
- 40 yards: 8 o'clock shot—lob wedge
- 50 yards: 9 o'clock shot—lob wedge
- 60 yards: 10 o'clock shot—lob wedge
- 70 yards: 10 o'clock shot—sand wedge
- 80 yards: 10 o'clock shot—pitching wedge
- 90–95 yards: full swing—lob wedge
- 105–110 yards: full swing—sand wedge
- 120–125 yards: full swing—pitching wedge

Each golfer's yardages will be slightly different, so go out and practice these shots and create a "yardage chart" for your own use.

Take any utility clubs, such as a gap wedge or any wedges that vary by only two or three degrees, out of your bag and add some utility woods. Women and senior golfers particularly benefit more from carrying a 7- or 9-wood than having four wedges in their bag. There are some new utility clubs on the market called Middleclubs, which have a heavy head and a significantly shorter shaft than the usual utility clubs. Ask for advice from your local golf school on obtaining these clubs.

Make sure that the gaps in loft between your wedges are equal for increased accuracy and lower scores. Have the gaps measured at a reputable golf store, and have them bend the clubheads a few degrees up or down if they are not quite right.

Choose the right wedges for your game and with a little bit of practice with these clubs, you will take several shots off that handicap.

Middleclubs have a heavy head and are shorter than the usual utility clubs. Replacing 2 and 3 irons with the 2 and 3 Middleclubs means you can hit the same distance, but with a club that is much easier to use.

# CHIPPING

A good chipping day can often compensate for a less-than-stellar ball-striking outing. Weekend golfers may not hit a ton of greens in regulation, but those that can get up and down from near the green will still score well. You can get yourself out of a lot of trouble with a good short game. Chipping is an especially enjoyable part of the game for the imaginative player because it provides the best opportunity to create shots with the least amount of risk. You can chip with a variety of clubs depending on your lie and path to the hole. The stroke itself is similar to a putting stroke, made with anything from a sand wedge to a 5-iron.

The weekend player often overlooks this part of the game. You may consider it more fun to bang driver after driver down the practice range but you are sadly mistaken. Chipping is one area every golfer can improve and it may be the easiest to improve because of the benign motions involved. It is also the area of your game that will most positively affect your score.

The golden rule in chipping is to fly the ball in the air as little as possible and roll the ball as much as possible. With that in mind, it is important to understand the air time/ground time ratios of shots hit with different clubs. The selection of the correct club is vital. You can chip with anything from a 3-iron to a sand wedge, depending on the situation, but you must know the following formulas to decide which club is required.

### The 6-8-10 Method for Chipping

When you chip with a 10-iron (or pitching wedge, as it is commonly called), the ball will fly half the distance to the hole and roll half the distance. When you chip with an 8-iron, the ball will fly a third and roll for two thirds. When you chip with a 6-iron, the ball will fly a quarter and roll for three-quarters.

These formulas are based on a normal-paced, level green (a situation we don't often find on the course), so if you are chipping uphill you would need to go up one club and if you are chipping downhill you need to go down one club. If the green is fast, again you will need to go down one club and if the green is slow you will go up one club. This may sound confusing at first, but once you understand the basic formula, it really is just common sense from then on.

| CLUB | LEVEL | UPHILL/SLOW | DOWNHILL/FAST |
|------|-------|-------------|---------------|
| 6-iron | Fly ¼; roll ¾ | 5-iron | 7-iron |
| 8-Iron | Fly ½; roll ½ | 7-iron | 9-iron |
| PW | Fly ½; roll ½ | 9-iron | SW |

The table opposite will help you understand the different clubs needed for various chipping situations. Remember, the landing spot is always about three feet to four feet onto the green.

### The Technique

At the address position, the weight is on the front foot, with the ball position in the middle of the feet. The hands are slightly ahead of the ball.

In order to land the ball on the correct spot, you need to make your practice swings looking at where you want to land the ball and not at the ground. By doing this, your subconscious will determine how hard you need to hit the ball to fly it in the air the correct distance.

By doing a backward and forward motion continually, called the "brush brush shot," you will eventually develop the feel necessary to fly the ball any distance you want (1 to 4).

### Setup/Swing

With your feet practically together, open up your stance relative to your target line. Play the ball off your back foot.

Your hands and your head should be set behind the ball and remain there throughout the entire stroke. Your hands go back low and finish low. Your goal is to keep the ball down and get it rolling quickly. It's an extension of a putt.

Choke down on the grip. Make a smooth stroke incorporating little wrist break. Do not decelerate through impact. Rhythm is the key.

103

### Important Aspects of Chipping

The most important aspect of chipping, besides choosing the right club, is to make sure that the left wrist (right wrist for left-handers) does not break down or bend during the chipping motion.

The moment the wrist breaks down, two things start to happen:

1. The loft on the club changes, therefore changing the trajectory, which, in turn, affects the roll of the ball. Inconsistent distances will result.

2. The arm bends as well, causing bladed shots that go screaming across the green.

To ensure that neither of these things happens, work on keeping your arm straight and your wrist firm during the shot. If you find this difficult to achieve in practice, try taking a thick rubber band and placing it around your wrist. Slide the butt end of the club under the rubber band, keeping the butt end of the club close to the wrist. This will give you the correct feel when chipping the ball.

If you wish to lower your handicap, skip a few sessions on the driving range, and head for the chipping green instead. You'll love the results to your game, but your opponents won't!

### Fairway Woods

Do not limit yourself to chipping only with specific clubs but rather use the right club for the right situation. If you are in fluffy grass around the green, try chipping with a 3- or 5-wood. The large soleplate will prevent the club from getting caught up in the grass and the loft will lift the ball over the fringe and get it rolling on the green fairly quickly. It is easy to have a high success rate with this shot without much practice (1 and 2).

### *The Bellied Wedge*

When the ball is sitting up against the fringe of the green, it is sometimes difficult to get the face on the ball. Use your sand wedge and strike the ball on the equator (3), causing the ball to roll away from the fringe smoothly (4). You should hit this shot as hard as you would have with your putter.

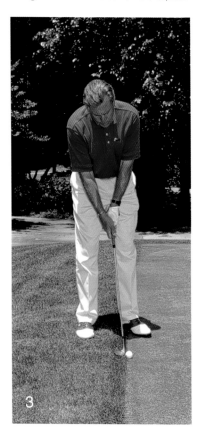

### The Texas Wedge

The Texas wedge refers to the use of your putter from off the green. They say that in Texas it is so windy, you have to keep the ball on the ground as much as possible. Use this shot when the fringe between you and the green is fairly smooth and the putting surface is fast.

Anytime you feel that it would be difficult landing the ball on the green with a chip and stop the ball at the flag, consider the Texas wedge. Remember to hit the putt a little firmer to compensate for going through the fringe.

The general rule of thumb is for every foot of fringe you have to putt through, add a foot to the distance of the putt. For

example, if you have a twenty-foot putt to make, and four feet of that distance is through the fringe, hit the putt as hard as you would hit a twenty-four foot putt.

This sequence of photographs shows the Texas wedge in action.

### Bump and Run

If it's possible for you to keep your ball near the ground, take advantage of this. Use a 6-iron or 7-iron and take a normal chipping stance.

Pick out a spot where you want to land the ball and focus on it. The bump and run is fundamentally a long, extended version of the putting stroke. Hit your shot as you would a putt. The decreased loft of a middle iron will allow the ball to roll upon landing. This high-percentage shot can save you.

### From Rough/Bellied

Heavy rough around the green can make it difficult to execute a normal chip. One option is to strike the ball with your wedge's leading edge.

Set the back of your wedge on top of the rough and treat the shot like a putt. You eliminate the possibility of snagging the club on the takeaway.

### 3-Wood Chip

Choke down on your 3-wood and take a normal chipping stance. Make a putting stroke and let the wood run the ball to the hole.

### *Chipping Drill*

The long shaft on this practice club helps ingrain the feeling of keeping your wrists steady through impact. Loose wrists increase the margin for error.

This drill forces you to keep the clubhead in line. When the hands are too involved, the clubhead tends to get manipulated inside or outside, which results in mishits.

### Practicing Your Chipping at Home

Another aspect of your short game that you can work on indoors is chipping. One of the big keys to chipping is feel. You can develop this while at home when you don't have time to go to the practice area.

Set up a spare piece of carpet (1). Place a small object (such as a business card) out about six feet away to mark a landing spot. Do the practice swing looking at the landing spot to get the feel of how hard you need to hit the ball (2).

You can also chip the ball and attempt to land it on the card. If you can perfect this at home, you will be able to land the ball where you want to on the golf course.

In addition, if you can understand the air time/ground time ratios of your clubs (see table on page 101), your chipping will definitely improve.

### Goals for Chipping Technique

Work on your technique to:

1. Perfect the execution of the chipping stroke.
2. Develop feel in order to hit the ball in the air the required distance.

# PUTTING

Jack Nicklaus, in his classic instruction book *Golf My Way*, calls putting "that other game." The inference is that green work is completely separate from everything you do to get there. This is frighteningly true. How frustrating is it when it takes you more strokes to roll the ball twenty feet than it did to fly it 365 yards to the green? For this and other reasons, putting is as mental an exercise as it is physical.

Good stroke mechanics will help you to become a solid putter. Variations are presented in the following pages. But it is confidence that defines the truly great putters.

When your putting is on, you can shave bunches of strokes off of an otherwise pedestrian round. When you're putting poorly, you can destroy a solid ball-striking day. Putting can be depressing and exhilarating, unforgiving and surprising, maddening and pleasant, but it is never boring.

The beginner may never be able to manufacture an intentional draw with his 4-iron, but, with enough practice, he can expect to get down in two from thirty-five feet. Sometimes the hole looks big—and sometimes you wonder if it's there at all.

### Green Reading

Begin reading the slope as you approach the green to determine drainage and overall pitch. Squat about three feet behind your ball.

Break your putts into three sections. Read the first third, the second third, and then the last third.

Most amateurs don't pay enough attention to the direction of the grain. When you get to the green, take the time to check the way the grass is growing. Your putts will move faster down grain and slower against the grain.

Read the break from behind your ball, then walk around to the other side of the pin, continually judging the slope. Squat opposite the ball and read again.

BELOW: *Reading the green: With the grain, the ball travels quickly. Against the grain, the ball runs slowly and falls short of the hole. Across the grain, the ball veers in the direction of the grain.*

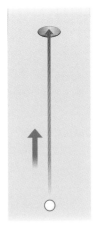

### Plumb Bobbing

This tricky technique involves squatting behind your ball while holding your putter about midshaft. Extend your arm out straight with your club straight up.

You must determine which of your eyes is dominant. Focus on an object and then close one eye. If the object moves, then your closed eye is dominant. That's the one to plumb bob with.

With your ball between your club and the hole, notice how much the green slopes relative to your shaft. Move to the opposite side and repeat.

Plumb bobbing is a very difficult, and often time-consuming, exercise to master. Beginners should practice the technique exhaustively before trying it on course.

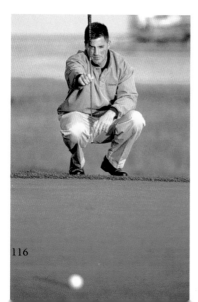

### Regular Putting Grip

Although there's no absolute right way to hold your putter, you'll be a better putter if you're comfortable holding the club.

Rest the shaft gently across the bottom pads of your left hand. Place your right hand below. Overlap your forefinger on top of your right hand.

### Left Hand Low/Cross

Some golfers reverse their hands, placing their left hand below their right (or vice versa). The idea is to take your wrists completely out of the stroke. This putting grip forces your right hand to remain solid and continue down the line of your putt. It also helps your wrists to remain firm.

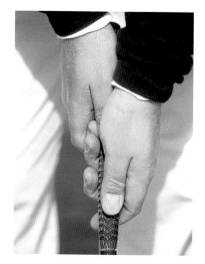

### Putting Posture

There is no single correct putting posture. If you follow the drills described here, and the putter head is traveling toward the target with the face square to your intended line, it matters less how you stand. However, here are a few postures that have worked well over the years for some great golfers.

Jack Nicklaus likes to crouch over his putts and uses more of a "piston" action with his right forearm to move the putter straight through (1).

Raymond Floyd likes to stand more upright, and in fact uses a slightly longer putter to allow himself to do this (2). He feels this posture allows him to see the line a lot better.

1

2

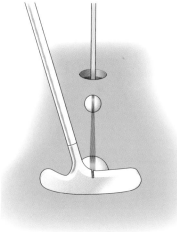

### Alignment

The single most important aspect of putting is alignment. Most golfers aim incorrectly, and the main reason for this is that our eyes are not designed to aim from a sideways position. All other sports that require aiming are face-on and therefore our eyes are focusing in a natural way. When we put our putter behind the ball, we get an optical illusion as to where we are aiming. This alignment can be as much as four inches to ten feet off.

The only way to line up correctly is to first put a stripe on your ball. A small plastic device designed for this purpose is available in most golf stores. Take the ball and draw a line halfway around the equator, making sure not to cover up the printing. Once you have established the correct line along which to putt, place the ball on the ground with the line on the ball along this target line.

Place your putter behind the ball, making sure that the line on the putter and the line on the ball are all on the same straight line.

Aim to play the ball in the middle of your stance with your knees slightly flexed. Your eyes should be directly over the ball.

LEFT: *The well-struck putt rolls the ball straight at the hole.*

### Ball Position

Play the ball about two inches inside your left heel (1), but move the ball forward if you have a severe downhill putt (2). This allows you to hit the ball with a little loft, giving a softer hit. Move the ball back in your stance for a severe uphill putt (3), which delofts the putter, imparting a little topspin on the ball and allowing you to get the ball up the slope without having to hit the ball quite as hard as you would from a normal position.

Now that you are aligned correctly and your ball is in the right position, go ahead and putt the ball. If the stroke is good, you should see the line on the ball rolling end over end. If this is not

happening, place a board along the outside of your putter to help you keep the putter head moving in a straight line toward the target.

### The Putting Stroke

You must be relaxed over the ball. Many golfers take a deep breath and exhale on takeaway. The most important aspect is good tempo. Focusing on keeping your head still will help you to hit the ball solid.

Bring the clubhead straight back or slightly inside and return it through the ball on exactly the same path.

### Long Putter Stroke

Hold the long putter with your left hand high and your right hand low to create a straight back/straight through pendulum motion.

The upright stance of the long putter can be more comfortable for golfers with bad backs. It also takes the wrists completely out of the stroke.

### *Lag Putting*

While you want to make every putt, it's critical to get your ball close with the first attempt. Three-putting is demoralizing.

Most amateurs will leave long putts short. Focus on getting your ball at least a foot past the hole. Good long putting requires a lot of practice.

125

### *Missing on the Amateur Side*

When you leave a breaking putt below the hole, it's referred to as "missing on the amateur side." Most golfers never read enough break.

Conversely, when you leave a putt above the hole it's referred to as "missing on the pro side." The reason is that professionals are more likely to read too much break.

## Putting Drills

### The Push Drill

The first drill is designed to help you kinesthetically feel the correct movement of the arms and hands throughout the putt. The overall objective is to allow absolutely no breakdown between the forearm of the leading arm and the putter shaft. This ensures a perfect pendulum stroke. It also helps tremendously with distance control because the hands are completely passive and will not get involved in hitting the ball, which causes loss of distance control. This drill takes six weeks to perfect, but you can practice at any time, at the office or at home, for just a few minutes a day.

Week 1

You need a straightedge of some kind in order to do this drill, such as a yardstick. Put the putter directly behind the ball (see 1 on following page). Without taking the clubhead back, simply push the head through, keeping the toe of the putter along the yardstick. The face stays at 90 degrees to the yardstick and the putter head is low to the ground (see 2 on following page). You do not need a target to aim at, just make sure you feel the upper part of the leading arm

controlling this movement and not the hands. The angle between the leading arm and the shaft should not change.

Week 2

Place the ball in the middle of the yardstick and place the putter six inches behind the ball. Now push the putter head through to twelve inches beyond where the ball was, making sure that you feel the upper part of the leading arm controlling the push with no breakdown between the forearm and the shaft. The toe of the putter must stay parallel to the ruler, and the face must remain square.

127

### Week 3

Finally, put all of this together by making a continuous putting stroke, still using the ruler and still taking the putter head back half the distance of the follow-through. Pay attention to detail and ensure that the toe of the putter stays on the yardstick and the putter face remains square 100 percent of the time. You won't derive any benefit from these drills if you do not pay attention to what the putter head is doing. Remember, in weeks 1, 2, and 3, there is no target, allowing you to focus strictly on the putting motion.

### Week 4

Go back to the same drill as week 1, but now use a target (3). If you're on a putting green, use the hole; if you are at home, use a putting cup.

### Week 5

Do the same drill as week 2, but also with a target. The target needs to be a little further away than it was in week 4.

### Week 6

Finally, do the same drill as in week 3 but with a target. The target needs to be a little further away than in week 5.

The reason you do not have a target for the first three weeks is to make you focus on what the putter head is doing and not what the ball is doing. If you had a target, your attention would be on seeing the ball go into the hole and the true focus of watching the putter head would be lost.

### Frequently Asked Questions

"Doesn't the push drill make you start to push your putts?"

It is important while doing the push drill that you use a ruler or something that will help you push the putter straight through. The toe of the putter must stay an equal distance from the ruler at all times. This way the putter head is always on-line. The face of the putter must at all times be at 90 degrees to the ruler in order for the ball to roll on the exact line you want.

"How does this drill work when putting normally?"

A drill is to be used only on the practice green so you can train yourself to repeat it competently over and over. In time, you won't have to think of the drill—you will automatically have a good putting stroke. Once you have chosen the line you can keep focused only on the speed needed to hit the putt, something all great putters do.

"I thought you weren't supposed to be right-hand dominant when you putted?"

The push drill is to help you feel the arm and hands kinesthetically through the putting stroke, and the objective is not to feel breakdown between the arms and hands. This means that there is no dominant hand or arm when you putt. By doing the push drill, you will finally feel the big muscles in the shoulders and upper back controlling the putting motion, eliminating the small muscles of the arms and hands, which are the real killers in the putting stroke.

Remember that each of the push drills needs to be practiced (either at home or on the putting green) for at least one week in order to develop a completely automatic motion.

### Repetitive Putt Drill

Short putts, those between four and six feet, are the ones we expect to make most of the time. Research shows that the touring pros make only about 50 percent of six foot putts, so the average golfer shouldn't get too frustrated when his or her percentage is lower. However, with intelligent practice, you can do something to increase that percentage.

### How to Practice

Take ten balls and line up a straight putt of about three to four feet using a straightedge to help ensure that the putter is moving straight back and through. You could also use a teaching aid (shown), which helps you keep the putterhead straight.

It is important to practice a straight putt, because then you need only focus on the stroke and not on the break. Obviously, if you miss a straight putt, you will know that you made a bad stroke. If you miss a breaking putt, you may have made a good stroke but just had the wrong speed. As we are working on the stroke here and not feel, pick a straight putt.

Now, start putting with two objectives:
1. Make sure the head is going straight back and straight through.
2. Make sure the face is square to your line at all times. This is the most common fault with poor putters and requires much work and concentration, but will have huge benefits if you have the determination to get it right.

Set yourself a goal for the number of putts that you can sink in a row. Gradually increase this goal until you can get up to fifty. Remember, if you miss one you have to start at number one again.

This teaches you how to putt under pressure, because as you get close to fifty, you don't want to start at one again—so you must make a good stroke.

The secondary benefit of this practice method is to your subconscious. As you sink putt after putt at this distance, your confidence escalates and you have less and less fear. If you don't have time to go to the course, you can practice this at home on the carpet. This is a great way to get your putting stroke solid for next spring, especially for those of you who are stuck indoors for the winter.

### Develop the Feel of a Pro

Usually, when we three-putt, it's because we have left the first putt either too long or too short. Rarely do we leave our first putt too wide, left or right of the hole. The reason for this is what is known as "lack of feel" for the shot.

What is this thing called feel? Is it something that exists in our hands? No, feel exists in your subconscious. Take a ball and throw it to a target; not only do you not think of your target distance in feet and inches, you don't consider how far back to take your hand to achieve this distance. This is because we grew up as kids throwing a ball and our subconscious knows exactly how hard to throw the ball to reach the target. So if you want to develop good feel as a golfer, you have to train your subconscious to know exactly how hard to hit your long putts.

### The Method

Set up about twenty balls and aim for a target about forty feet away (1). Once you have lined up, putt the ball at the target, looking at the hole and not at the ball (2).

This may feel a little strange at first, but you'll soon get used to it. Remember, do not look at the ball when you putt, look at the hole. If you hit your first putt too soft (2), then hit your next putt a little harder (3), still looking at the hole. If you hit that putt too soft, then hit the next one a little

harder (4). Continue this with each ball until you get the feel for exactly how hard to hit the putt (5).

Once you have hit all the balls to your target, pick a new target and start all over again. Remember though, this is a practice drill for the putting green only. When you are on the course, take your practice swings looking at the target, but once you are lined up, look at the ball to ensure solid contact with the center of the face.

### Putting with Your Left Arm

Putting only with your left arm forces you to concentrate on controlling your stroke on a steady path. It also helps to discourage the use of wrists and hands in the putting motion.

Putting with one arm trains you to keep your body very still, which, in turn, helps you to hit the ball solidly.

### *Tee Putting*

Place a tee at the point where your putt breaks and putt only to the tee. This drill helps you hone distance control skills.

Putting to a tee on a breaking putt helps you to read the green. You'll also develop a more thorough understanding of how slopes affect roll.

### Railroad Track Putting

Lay two clubs behind your putter head parallel to each other. This "railroad track" helps you to visualize the straight back/straight through path.

Most inexperienced putters will bring the clubhead outside the line and cut it coming through. This drill encourages topspin as opposed to sidespin.

### Clock Drill

Place three balls equidistant from the hole on four sides. You must make all three at each station before moving on to the next.

This clock drill is excellent for building putting confidence. It helps to familiarize you with the feeling and visualization of the ball going in the hole.

# SAND PLAY

Men like Gary Player and Seve Ballesteros are famous for their uncanny ability to extract the ball from the greenside bunker and deposit it near or in the hole. Many PGA Tour players would rather play from a bunker than longish rough nearby. However, greenside bunkers are not as difficult as most amateur players believe. The problem is, generally, that most beginners haven't learned the proper technique of escape.

Fairway bunkers are a different story. Course designers include them to penalize a wayward shot. There are several factors involved that make fairway bunkers extremely difficult. First you must overcome the mental anguish of just having hit your ball so off-line that it ended up there in the first place. Then you must negotiate whatever lip might exist and gauge the distance required for a ball not sitting on grass.

In the next few pages you'll learn how to increase your odds of getting greenside bunker shots close and how to survive bunkers out in the fairway.

### Setup/Swing

For a greenside blast, open your body to the target line and play the ball back in your stance. An open stance will help you get your body through the ball. Choke down on the club.

Focus on a spot one inch behind your ball. Swing along your shoulder line and strike that spot. Pick up the clubhead abruptly on your takeaway to facilitate a downward blow at impact. This gives your ball height and lands it soft.

The club will propel sand and your ball high and softly. Make sure your clubface points at your target.

139

### Greenside Bunker Shot

Using your sand wedge, set up with your feet slightly open to the target, the clubface slightly open, and your weight set mostly on your front foot. Aiming about two inches behind the ball, swing the clubhead back and through along the intended line, making sure to finish the swing (see the following pages).

Two of the most critical components of this shot are first, to make sure that your left arm does not break down, and second, to control the shot with your body rotation, not with your arms. The most common mistake golfers make in the bunker is to try and scoop the ball out,

resulting in the left arm breaking down and the weight moving toward the back foot. This produces either a sculled shot or the club enters the sand too far behind the ball, causing the clubhead to decelerate and the ball to remain in the bunker.

The bunker shot is just another pitch shot, so control your distance in the same way as you would a pitch shot. However, as you are hitting two inches behind the ball, the ball will obviously not go as far as with a pitch shot. The general rule of thumb is that the ball goes about half the distance. So if your 9 o'clock pitch shot went 50 yards, your 9 o'clock bunker shot will go about 25 yards.

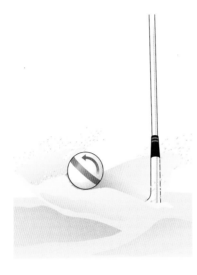

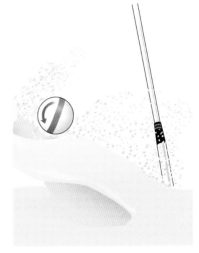

*Sand Play in Profile:*

CLOCKWISE FROM TOP LEFT:
*Psychological lift. Don't ground the club or touch the ball.*
*Splash down. Accelerate down smoothly.*
*Back spinner. Feel the club sliding down and under the ball.*
*Sandblast. Keep up clubhead momentum.*
*Heading for safety. The clubhead leaves a shallow trough in the sand as the ball is propelled toward the target.*

3

4

7

8

When you first start working on bunker shots, draw a line in the sand about two inches behind the ball, and practice hitting that line consistently. This is an absolute must if you want to become a good bunker player. If you are hitting too far behind the ball, chances are you are starting your downswing with your arms and not with body rotation. Starting the downswing with the arms is an absolute no-no. If you have rotated your body correctly, you will finish the swing with all your weight on your front foot, your arms extended out in front of you, and your belt buckle facing the target. Work toward this end, and you will become a consistent player out of the sand. This sequence of pictures shows the greenside bunker shot in profile.

### Fairway Bunkers

Fairway bunkers are installed by architects for one of two reasons. They either want to make the hole more difficult or they want to add aesthetic value to the hole. In either case, fairway bunkers are best avoided. However, we have all been in a fairway bunker at one time or another, so it is important to understand how to play from these hazards.

The bunkers in North America are generally fairly shallow and allow golfers to

advance the ball either well down the fairway or onto the green. In countries such as Scotland and Ireland, fairway bunkers are much deeper and present more of a problem if you venture into one. It sometimes requires a sideways shot to extricate oneself from them.

Once you are in the bunker, you have to decide which club you are going to use. Obviously the distance to your target is a deciding factor; the other factor is the height of the front lip of the bunker. In order to decide the choice of club, stand outside the bunker, lay your club flat on the ground, and stand on the clubface. The resulting shaft angle will give you an approximate trajectory of the ball with that particular club. You can then decide whether that club will get the ball safely over the lip of the bunker. It is far better to take a more lofted club and come up a little short of your target than to use a less lofted club and end up burying the ball in the face of the bunker.

With your chosen club, take your normal stance and play the ball very slightly further back in your stance. Do not dig your feet into the sand as you would in a greenside bunker, as this will put your feet slightly lower than the ball, causing a tendency to hit behind the ball and having it come up short of the target.

Try to make as smooth a swing (1 and 2) as possible so that your feet do not slip, and finish with a full follow-through with all your weight on your front foot (3).

Any attempt to scoop the ball in order to get it up will cause the clubhead to enter the sand behind the ball and a "fat" shot will result.

### Playing to a Close Flagstick

When the flagstick is really close and you need to stop the ball in a hurry, a slightly different technique is necessary. The best thing to use is a 60-degree lob wedge for this shot. Open the clubface and position yourself in a slightly open stance. Take the clubhead outside the target line on the backswing (1 and 2) and hit only one inch behind the ball with a slight cutting motion (3, 4, and 5). This will give the ball both height and spin and will allow it to stop very quickly (6 and 7). This is a shot that requires a lot of practice, as hitting only one inch behind the ball allows for only a very small margin of error.

**1**

**4**

**5**

2

3

6

7

### Ball Near Face of Bunker

This is a shot that often intimidates people, but again, the correct technique will always get the ball out. Open the clubface, make a bigger swing than normal, and make sure to follow through. Do not let the bank in front of your ball make you stop your follow-through. Again, a little practice to develop confidence in the shot and the understanding that it must be played aggressively will lead to better shots in this situation in the future.

### Buried Lie in Bunker

The buried lie in a bunker is an easier shot than most people think. Instead of opening the clubface, this time you must close it so that the clubface is aiming toward your front toe. The secret to this shot is to make sure that your grip pressure is very loose. Still hit two inches behind the ball. As the toe of the club enters the sand it digs in because of the closed clubface. However, because of the loose grip, the force of the sand will twist the club slightly in your hands squaring the clubface off and popping the ball out of the sand. This ball will land with a lot of topspin so plan to land this ball well short of the hole.

### Long Pitch from Bunker

This is one of the most difficult shots in golf, as there is no margin for error. It is played exactly the same as a normal pitch shot with one exception. The ball position is played slightly back of center in order to allow the hands to pass the ball early in the downswing (1). This enables the clubhead to hit the ball with a fairly steep descending blow. Follow through in the normal manner (2). Control distance with your 7, 8, or 9 o'clock backswing. The ball trajectory will be a little lower but with plenty of backspin, so the ball should still go the same distance as a regular pitch shot. Do not attempt to pick this shot clean off the sand as you will have a tendency to hit slightly behind the ball, leaving it short of your target and sometimes still in the sand. Pictures 3 to 6 show the pitch shot in profile.

151

1

### Ball in Back of Bunker

When the ball is in the back of the bunker, the back edge can hinder the takeaway and downswing. By using a "tomahawk shot," you can extricate the ball fairly easily. Address the ball with one foot outside the bunker (1) and start the takeaway almost vertically (2, 3, and 4). This will eliminate the back edge of the bunker. Bring the club back down to the ball on this vertical plane and let the club enter the sand about two inches behind the ball (5, 6, and 7). "Chicken wing" your left arm, pulling the clubhead across the ball. The result is a fairly high, soft shot coming out of the bunker with quite a bit of left-to-right spin, so aim well left of the hole (8, 9, and 10).

2

3

6

9

10

### Upslope in Sand

For this shot, set your shoulders at the same angle as the slope. Choke down, making an aggressive stroke, and bury your clubhead into the slope just below your ball.

Treat your wedge as a shovel to get the ball out. Use some extra grip pressure because you'll be chopping down pretty violently. Most importantly, remember that it's the sand that propels the ball out, not the clubface.

### Downslope in Sand

Set your shoulders at the same angle as the slope. Follow the slope's angle back and through, working to strike the ball first.

Try to imagine you're peeling the bottom part of the cover off the ball.

### Long Blast

The greenside blast technique can be used from farther away with lower lofted clubs. Be sure you use a club with enough loft to clear any lip. Choke down enough on your club relative to how much you dig your feet in the sand.

### *Firm, Wet Sand*

The bounce built into your sand wedge requires you to clip the ball from this situation, rather than attempting a normal blast. It's crucial to strike the sand firmly behind the ball—do not hit it thin.

### *Sand Practice*

Bury a short board so that the sand just covers it. Practice your splash technique to get a feeling for the bounce involved. Beginners find this drill ideal for gauging just how much sand is needed to get the ball out of the greenside bunker. This should help you to become familiar with the proper peeling motion while improving your confidence.

Bury four balls in progressively difficult lies. Hit the exposed ball first. As the ball buries farther under the sand, it will come out with less spin and roll more once on the green. You will need to take this into consideration and attempt to land it accordingly.

# HAZARDS AND
# TROUBLE SHOTS

How pleasant golf would be if every ball sat proudly up in the fairway, invitingly ready to be struck. As you know, more often than not, the ball huddles dourly in some sort of less-than-ideal spot, daring you to hack it out. The lie of the ball dictates how you must attack it. Most of the instruction thus far has been directed toward strokes made at a ball sitting in the fairway or light rough. Now you'll learn what to do in circumstances that are less fortunate.

How often have you wondered to yourself, "Is there a single even lie on this course?" Balls lying uphill, downhill, and sidehill are some of the most tricky to overcome. Equally as frustrating are balls in a divot, balls in heavy rough, balls on bare spots, etc. All of these and more will be covered in the following pages. There are also suggestions for thoughtful course management and club selection, depending on your lie. Learning how to execute the trouble shots is important for making them less troublesome.

### *Hitting off Hardpan*

Treat hardpan in the same way as a regular fairway shot, with one exception. If you are playing an iron shot, the normal ball position on the fairway is two inches inside your left heel (1 and 2). Off hardpan the ball position is directly off your left heel, allowing you to catch the ball right at the bottom of the arc, almost like a fairway wood. This allows you to "clip" the ball off hardpan without hitting a divot. If you hit down too steeply on hardpan the club might jar and you could injure yourself.

# Draws and Fades

When faced with an obstacle such as a tree in front, your option is to go under, over, left, or right of the tree. As the green is 250 yards away, under is not an option, and neither is over, as you could not get your shot with the 3-wood up in the air fast enough. Your choices are to either fade the ball down the left side or draw the ball down the right side. If you aim to the right over the hazard and the ball does not draw, the ball will end up in the hazard. If you aim to the left and the ball does not fade, the ball will end up out of bounds, which is even worse. The correct shot to play is the one you feel most confident in.

### Hitting an Intentional Draw

First aim your feet, hips, and shoulders slightly to the right of your target (1). Start your backswing by taking the club back a little more inside the target line than normal, causing you to have a slightly flatter backswing (2). Start the downswing by dropping your hands straight down and keeping them very close to the body. Make sure you exaggerate the inside-out action of the clubhead, at the same time allowing your hands to roll over through the hitting area.

Stay down on this shot (3), as an early straightening of the spine will prevent the correct release and the ball will be left out to the right. If you have confidence in your ability to draw the ball, be totally committed to the shot. You will be rewarded with a nice, high draw.

BELOW: *The draw. Aim the club right of the target and align your body right of the ball-to-target line.*

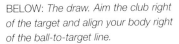

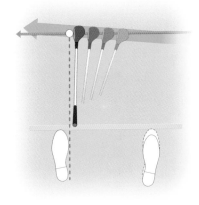

### Hitting an Intentional Fade

Start out by aiming your feet, hips, and shoulders to the left of the target (1). Start the backswing by taking the clubhead slightly outside the target line, creating a fairly steep backswing (2).

Start the downswing with an early clearing of the left side, which will cause an outside-in clubhead path. Hold off releasing the hands for as long as possible, which will create a nice, high fade (3 and 4). As with the draw shot, be totally committed and trust your swing to create the shot.

BELOW: *High fade. Attack the ball with a steeper than normal downswing.*

NORMAL SWING PLANE

OUT-TO-IN PLANE

167

### Playing Left-handed Shots

For right-handed players this is a really great shot to have in your arsenal when you find yourself against a tree where a left-handed shot is required. With a little practice, you will be able to advance the ball a reasonable distance instead of taking a penalty drop. Choose a club like a pitching wedge or 9-iron (because they have a larger face), flip the club over so that the toe is pointing to the ground, and address the ball in a left-handed manner (1). Keep the backswing short, making sure that you keep the right arm straight throughout the shot (2). This creates a perfect arc, which will ensure that the clubface gets back to the ball squarely (3).

This shot needs to be practiced on the driving range before you ever try it on the golf course. However, the work is worth it, as it will save many strokes over the years.

### Playing Out of Heavy Rough

When playing out of heavy rough, your first objective should be to get the ball back into play. Advance the ball to an area that will make the next shot an easy one to the green. Depending on the height of the rough, choose a club with enough loft to get the ball airborne easily. With this particular shot, you want to use a fairly tight grip, particularly with the last three fingers of the left hand (1). Out of heavy rough, the clubface will have a tendency to shut down as the grass wraps around the hosel, so a firm grip will help prevent this. On the backswing, you want to have a fairly quick wrist cock so that the grass does not catch the clubhead (2 and 3). You also want to produce a fairly steep downswing so that the clubhead gets to the ball as quickly as possible (4). Make sure you keep the club moving through the grass by maintaining a good body rotation through the impact area to a full follow-through (5 and 6).

Once your club gets snarled in the thick rough, it has a tendency to turn, so you'll need to have a firm grip on the club. Take a comfortably firm stance when you're in pine needles because your feet are likely to slip and slide around during your swing.

### Playing Out of Water

If the ball is not completely submerged, but is lying just under the surface of water, then a shot can be played. Play it just like a bunker shot, aiming about two inches behind the ball and swinging about twice as hard as a regular bunker shot (1 to 8). A towel tucked in at the belt will prevent water and mud from soiling your clothes. This shot must be played aggressively, and, as with any bunker shot, a full follow-through is critical (9 to 11).

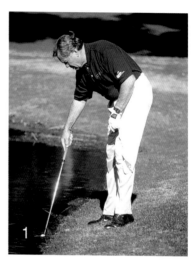

BELOW: *The water shot. At least half of the ball must be clear of the water to produce a successful shot.*

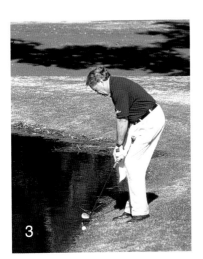

7

10

11

# Uphill and Downhill Lies

Most students, including low handicap players, are confused as how to play the ball from uphill and downhill lies. This uncertainty often results in bad shots. So let's set out a few principles.

### Uphill Lies

The ball position needs to be forward in the stance and your body tilted almost perpendicular to the slope (1). Most of your weight should be on your back foot (2) as you make the shot.

After completing the shot, your weight should still be on your back foot (3). This is one of the few shots in golf where there is no weight shift. If you try to shift your weight to the front foot, you will raise your body and top the ball.

A few tips to remember:

• Take at least one extra club (a 7-iron instead of an 8), or maybe two if the slope is a severe one.

• Aim to the right (for right-handed golfers), as the tendency is to pull the ball.

• On uphill or downhill lies, always play the ball off your highest foot (in this case the front foot).

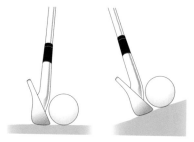

ABOVE: *Increased loft from upslope.*

BELOW: *5-iron from level lie.*

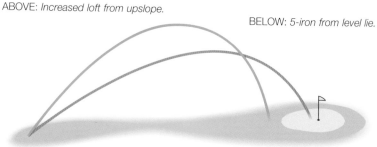

### Downhill Lies

The ball should be positioned back in your stance and your body tilted almost perpendicular to the slope (1). Most of your weight should be on your front foot.

If the ball was positioned incorrectly toward the front foot, you would tend to hit behind the ball, as the ground behind the ball is higher than the ball.

The follow-through is shortened (3). If you were to follow through all the way, the momentum would pull you off balance.

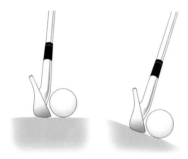

ABOVE: *Reduced loft from downslope.*

BELOW: *5-iron from level lie.*

GOLF SKILLS

A few tips to remember:

• Take one club less (an 8 instead of a 7) and play the ball off the back foot, which decreases the loft and increases distance.

• Aim to the left (for right-handed golfers), as the ball will tend to fade.

• On uphill or downhill lies, always play the ball off your highest foot (in this case the back foot).

### Ball Below the Feet

A ball below your feet on a sidehill lie is the most difficult of all sloping lies. Do not bend your knees too much in order to reach the ball. This will tend to make you rise up as you swing through, causing you to top the ball. Keep your legs at their normal flex and bend over more from the waist (1). As long as you maintain your spine angle, you will not rise up (2 and 3).

A few tips to remember:

• Sustain your normal knee flex and bend a little more from the waist.

• Keep the backswing short. If you try to swing to your normal position, there will be a tendency to rise up.

BELOW: *Ball below feet. Flex your knees more than usual and bend from the waist to ensure a good shot. Placing the ball further back in your stance will help to avoid a thin shot.*

• Take one more club (an 8 instead of a 9). Aim to the left, as the ball will have a tendency to fade or go to the right (for right-handed golfers).

*GOOD SHOT*

*THIN SHOT*

### Ball Above the Feet

When the ball is above your feet, in order to keep your normal posture, you must grip the club a little shorter. If you do not, the club will hit the ground first. Straightening the body and especially the legs, to compensate for the club feeling too long, will tend to make you lose your balance very easily—something you do not want at any time.

A few tips to remember:

• Take one club more (a 7 instead of an 8) and play the ball off the middle of your stance.

• Aim to the right (for right-handed golfers), as the ball will tend to hook or pull.

• Grip the club shorter. The amount of slope will determine how much shorter to grip; a greater slope means a shorter grip to make sure you are in your normal posture.

• Make as smooth a swing as possible. Don't try and pull the ball back in line, as it will do that on its own.

### Steep Slopes

Stance can be a major problem, as the slopes tend to throw you backward, making you lose your balance. Or, if your weight is on your back foot when you play the shot, you'll sometimes tend to scuff behind the ball. Place your back foot at 90 degrees to the shot, either in the bunker or on the slope, and place your front foot perpendicular to the slope (1). This lets your left knee move out of the way and allows you to lean your body forward, putting weight on the ball of your front foot. Your hands stay ahead of the clubhead, allowing you to make clean contact with the ball and maintain your balance throughout the shot (2 to 6).

# High Shots

### Club Selection

To hit the ball high over an obstacle, such as a tree or bush, you must first select a club with enough loft to get you over the obstacle. Lay the club you have selected down on the ground and stand on the clubface. The shaft angle produced will give you an approximate trajectory of that particular club.

### Ball Position

The ball should be two inches further forward than usual at the address position (1).

### Weight Distribution

Your weight should be slightly toward your back foot, with your back shoulder lower than normal and your hands very slightly behind the clubhead. Stand behind the ball and visualize the trajectory going easily over the tree or bush and landing safely at your target.

### The Shot

Take a normal backswing, and on the follow-through, keep the club low through the hitting area and finish with a nice, high follow-through (2). This swing should produce a higher than normal trajectory.

185

# Low Shots

### Club Selection

You need to select a club with very little loft, perhaps a 4- or 5-iron. (Do not select a 2- or 3-iron, because the ball position is back and there is not enough loft on these clubs to get the ball airborne.)

### Ball Position

The ball should be back in the stance, with the hands well ahead of the clubhead (1).

### Follow-through

The follow-through must be short and straight through to the target (6 and 7). (A long, full follow-through will result in a higher trajectory.)

### Key Factors

Set the weight forward while executing the shot. Make sure that the left arm stays absolutely straight through impact (2 to 5). The slightest breakdown of the left arm will cause the clubhead to overtake the hands, and the ball will immediately go higher and crash into those overhanging branches.

This shot takes a little practice, so experiment with different clubs and see just how low and far you can hit the ball. It will pay dividends on the course.

GOLF SKILLS

### *Tree Shots*

Creativity comes to the fore when negotiating these terrible lies. Whether bouncing off the trunk or flipping around left-handed, concentrate on smoothness.

Play the ball back as far in your stance as possible to give yourself the maximum room to swing through the ball.

### *Rain Play*

As uncomfortable as rain play can be, the most important aspect of surviving the water is to impact the ball first. Any shot hit fat is impossible.

You may want to squat a little more in your stance to feel grounded and firm. Always take an extra club so you can choke down and swing smoothly while still getting enough distance. You won't swing as hard if you know you have more club in your hands.

# PROBLEM SOLVING

Some of the most common faults in golf can be easily solved once the golfer has analyzed his problem and made the appropriate changes. This section offers solutions to some of the most familiar problems experienced by golfers.

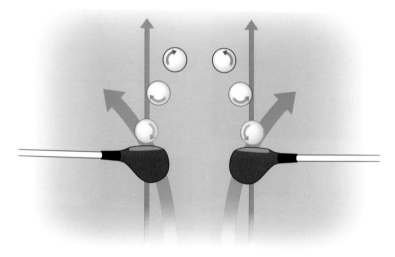

## Slicing

ABOVE: *Slicing—right-handed and left-handed.*

When the ball curves significantly from left to right (for right-handed golfers), slicing occurs. Slicing is caused by the clubhead path cutting across the ball from the outside in. The clubface angle is open at impact, imparting spin on the ball and causing it to veer off-line. As there are several swing flaws that can cause a slice, each one will be addressed separately.

GOLF SKILLS

**1**

Fault: Starting the backswing with the clubhead moving outside the target line. The hands move away from the body line, causing the clubhead to move outside the target line on the backswing (1).

Halfway down the downswing, the hands are too far away from the body and the clubhead is outside the hands, ensuring an outside-in clubhead path (2).

**2**

The resulting downswing will cause the clubhead to finish low across the body, producing a slice (3). From the front angle, notice that the hands have finished below shoulder level (4). This is a sure sign of a pull or a slice.

In summary, when you start the clubhead outside the target line, it causes the backswing to become too steep, which then causes the hands to move away from the body on the downswing. The clubhead gets outside the hands on the downswing and finally the clubhead cuts across the ball with the follow-through finishing low across the body.

Cure: Start the backswing keeping the clubhead slightly outside the hands (5). Halfway up the backswing, make sure the shaft is pointing either at the ball or slightly inside (6). The downswing is started with a lateral slide of the hips, keeping the clubhead behind the hands as long as possible (7). The hands must travel down the body line in order for the clubhead path to stay on-line.

3

4

5

6

7

Make sure the hands move straight back along the body line and complete the backswing with your torso (and not your arms), which will allow the club to swing back on plane (8). (The backswing plane is a line drawn from the ball through the shoulders). The downswing is started with a lateral slide of the hips, ensuring that the clubhead stays behind the hands on the way down. This will produce an inside-out clubhead path on a line that allows the club to travel more toward the target, producing a straighter shot.

**9**

**8**

Fault: The right elbow has drifted away from the body, causing the backswing to become too steep (9).

Allowing the right elbow to drift away from the body on the backswing causes the right forearm to get into a horizontal position at the top of the backswing. This causes the downswing to become too steep, which in turn causes the clubhead to cut across the ball and produce a slice.

Cure: At the top of the backswing the right arm should be in a "tray" position (10). Make sure the right arm folds on the backswing, keeping the elbows the same distance apart as they were at address. The forearm finishes at the top of the swing more perpendicular to the ground, like a waiter carrying a tray. This allows the arms to drop down, keeping the clubhead behind the hands and producing an inside-out path.

Work on taking the club back correctly, making sure the right forearm is in the correct position and the left arm is on plane. Start the downswing with a lateral slide of the hips, which will allow the club to drop down, keeping the clubhead behind the hands. Finally, make sure the clubhead stays in line to the target for as long as possible through impact and allow the hands to release through the shot in order to square the clubface.

10

**1**

**2**

## Pulling

When the ball flies left of your target line, this is known as pulling.

Fault: Pulling happens when the clubhead path is moving from the outside in, but the clubface angle is square to the path. The ball travels in a straight line, but misses the target to the left. This is caused by one of two things.

The downswing is started with the upper body, causing the clubhead to move outside the hands on the downswing, resulting in an outside-in clubhead path (1). Or, the left hip rotates too soon as the downswing is started, again causing the clubhead to move outside the hands.

As the hands move through the impact position, they rotate, squaring the clubface angle to the clubhead path, and a straight pull will be the result (2).

Cure: Start the downswing with a lateral slide of the hips, allowing the hands to drop down close to the body (3). The clubhead stays behind the hands, the clubhead path moves more from the inside, and the arms travel down the body line (4).

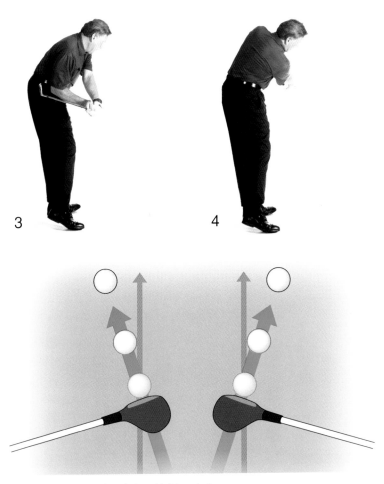

ABOVE: *Pulling—right-handed and left-handed.*

# Hooking

When the ball curves strongly from right to left (for right-handed golfers), it is known as hooking. There are two types of hooking faults, the push hook and the pull hook.

### Push Hook

Fault: The push hook is a shot that starts out to the right and moves back to the target, and a pull hook starts left and curves even further to the left.

The push hook results from the clubhead traveling too severely from the inside to out and the hands rotating too quickly. This is caused by the backswing starting out too flat (1) and the club shaft being laid off on the backswing (2).

This enables the clubhead to get too far on the inside on the downswing, forcing the club to strike the ball in a severe inside-out motion. Combined with the wrist rotation, the ball moves out to the right of the target and then hooks back severely.

**1**

**2**

**3**

Cure: Make sure to swing the club back on the correct plane (3) so that on the downswing, the clubhead is slightly behind the hands (4), which allows the clubhead to travel more directly down the line toward the target (5). This position might produce a slight draw, which is desirable. Stay in the correct posture throughout the sequence and don't let your eyes follow the ball until it is well on its way to the hole.

**4**

**5**

### Pull Hook

Like the slice, the pull hook, sometimes called a duck hook, is a totally undesirable shot. The ball starts off left of the target and hooks even further left, usually landing in trouble.

Fault: The pull hook is usually caused by a spin-out of the left hip, causing the shoulders to overrotate and the arms to be thrown away from the body (1 and 2). The clubhead path comes from outside-in. If the hands rotate through impact, the combination of clubhead path and clubface angle will cause the ball to start left and hook even further left. There is a saying in golf, "You can talk to a slice, but a hook won't listen."

Cure: Make sure the downswing is started with the hips and not with the arms (3). If the left hip initiates the downswing and moves laterally toward the target for the first few inches, the hands will drop down close to the body, keeping the clubhead slightly behind the hands, which allows the clubhead path to work more down the target line (4). This is a sure-fire way to prevent a pull hook.

# *Pushing*

**3**

The pushed shot is one that starts off straight right of the target without any curve.

Fault: The push shot is the closest to being a good swing without the ball hitting the target. Most elements of the golf swing are correct during a push shot with one exception—the hands fail to release, leaving the clubface slightly open. Even though the clubhead path has the desired inside-out motion, the ball will travel to the right. In the shot below, the clubface is still

**4**

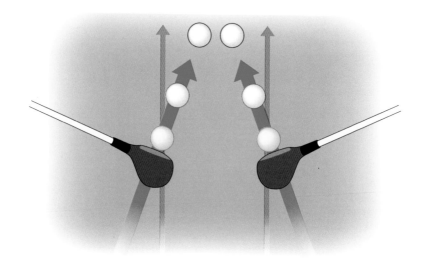

ABOVE: *Pushing—right-handed and left-handed.*

facing toward the sky instead of the toe pointing up, indicating a lack of rotation of the left forearm.

Cure: Make sure the hands release through the hitting area and that halfway through the follow-through the toe of the club is pointing toward the sky (see left). This ensures a square clubface position at impact.

# Topping

Topping is caused by either a change of spine angle or collapsing the left arm through impact. In both instances the bottom of the arc will be above the ball and a topped shot will result.

Fault: Topping is striking the middle or top half of the ball with the leading edge of the club, causing the ball to bounce along the ground without any airtime at all (1 and 2). Almost all beginners tend to top the ball

BELOW: *"Lifting" the ball causes topping.*

1

2

**3**

**4**

**5**

because they lack understanding of the true principles of ball striking.

Cure: When you are in your address position, you are X number of inches from the ball. This X is made up by the length of the shaft, the length of your left arm, and your spine angle at address.

Any change in either the length of the left arm or spine angle will cause a topped shot. To prevent this from happening, make sure that you keep your left arm straight throughout the swing and your spine angle in the same position as your address position (3 and 4) when you swing through the ball (5).

# *Overswinging*

Many golfers think that overswinging occurs when the club shaft reaches beyond parallel at the top of the backswing, but this is not necessarily the case. There is a specific top of the backswing position for each golfer and this will mainly depend on the golfer's level of flexibility. A golfer who is extremely flexible, like John Daly who gets the club well beyond parallel at the top of the swing and still maintains a straight left arm and a restricted hip turn, is still well in control of the swing. On the other hand,

someone like Doug Sanders, who had a short backswing, managed to hit the ball a long way and win many tournaments.

Fault: Overswinging happens when the left arm collapses at the top of the backswing or the hips overrotate (1). This means a loss of torque at the top of the backswing, which creates the speed on the downswing and follow-through.

Cure: Make sure the left arm is fully extended at the top of the backswing,

creating plenty of space between the right shoulder and hands (2). This also limits the amount of hip turn so that tightness is felt in the torso.

Fault: Letting go at the top. Another reason for overswinging is letting go of the last three fingers of the left hand at the top of the backswing (3). If your glove is continually getting worn out in the pad area, you are probably letting go at the top.

Cure: Keep the last three fingers of the left hand firmly on the club at the top of the backswing (4).

3

4

1

## Reverse Pivot

The reverse pivot is another swing flaw that is created by overswinging, trying to take the club back too far in an attempt to hit the ball further.

In fact the opposite occurs as the weight tends to move to the back foot on the downswing, causing the golfer to hit behind the ball. Releasing the hands too early on the downswing means hitting the ball on the upswing with a resulting loss of power. A good turn is critical if distance is a problem in your golf swing.

Fault: The spine angle tilts toward the target, leaving the weight on the front foot (1 and 2). This usually causes the back leg to straighten, which in turn causes the back hip to rise up, making it difficult to start the downswing with a good weight shift, as the weight is already on the front foot.

Cure: Get into your golf posture, leaning forward slightly from the waist and keeping your spine straight. Place a club along the inside of your back foot. This will act as a guide when you turn. Hold a club across your shoulders, making sure it is straight to get the correct alignment. (See 3 on following page.)

2

207

3

4

Make a shoulder turn until the club across your shoulders is over the club inside your back heel and pointing in the same direction (4). You will feel that the weight has now moved onto the back foot with most of the weight toward the back heel. This position will give you a proper feel for where you need to be at the top of the backswing. Now take the club that was across your shoulders and swing back until you feel you are in a similar position to where you were during the drill (5). From this position, you will have plenty of coil, which allows you to start your downswing with a good weight shift, enabling you to hit the ball a lot further.

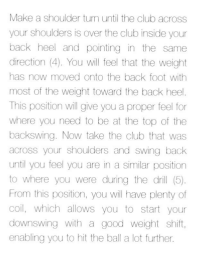

5

# *Errors in the Address Position*

The address position is vitally important to the start of a good golf swing. The correct address position includes a good posture, good knee flex, arms hanging comfortably from the body, and hands placed in the correct position (1 and 2).

Fault: A stance that is too narrow can cause poor balance on both the backswing and the follow-through (see 3 on following page).

Cure: Without the necessary balance, you cannot produce good shots, so widen your stance a little.

Fault: A wide stance is adopted by golfers who try to hit the ball a long way (see 4 on following page). Their theory is that a wide stance will give them good stability and therefore they will be able to put a hard swing on the ball.

**1**

**2**

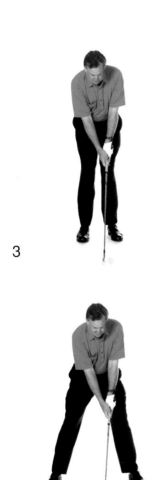

**3**

**4**

Cure: The opposite is true, as a wide stance restricts both the shoulder turn on the backswing and a good weight shift on the follow-through, which will hinder distance. A narrower stance is advisable.

Fault: When the ball gets too far back in the stance (5), it creates a backswing that is too steep, which results in the downswing also being too steep. This causes you to hit down on the ball, resulting in a low trajectory with iron shots and makes you pop up your tee shots.

Cure: Make sure the ball position is correct depending on the club you have.

Fault: When the hands get too far behind the ball (6), there is a tendency to start the backswing by cocking the wrists too early.

Cure: You want your arms, shoulders, and club to move in one motion, so it is important to have a straight line formed by your left arm and shaft all the way from the shoulder to the clubhead.

Fault: When your hands are too far ahead of the ball, it immediately puts your body out of position to make a good takeaway (7). The shoulders are forced into an open position and this address position usually causes the golfer to cut across the ball, producing a slice.

5

6

7

8

Cure: Again, make sure that the left arm and shaft form a straight line from your shoulder to the ball.

Fault: When the golfer stands too far from the ball, it makes the spine bend too far over. (See 8 on previous page.) This causes a change in spine angle on the backswing and the golfer raises his head to make a proper turn. On the downswing, the golfer will attempt to get back down to the ball to make solid contact. However, this up-and-down motion leads to inconsistency in ball striking.

9

Cure: From your address position, take your right hand off the club, make a fist, and place the fist between the top of your left thigh and the butt of the club (9). This is a good guide to tell you how far your hands should be from your body in the address position.

Fault: Standing too close to the ball. When a golfer stands too close to the ball (10), there is a tendency to take the club away on a steep plane, causing them to cut across the ball on the downswing, producing a pull or a slice depending on where the hands are at impact.

10

Cure: Again, use the "fist rule" (9) to gauge the correct distance from the ball in the address position.

# Gaining Power: Keeping Accuracy

Many golfers who attempt to add distance to their drives suddenly find that they have lost the accuracy they once had. Can you retain accuracy if you try to add power? The answer is definitely yes.

Often, golfers believe they have to increase the length of the backswing in order to add power. This creates additional problems, which can end up costing them distance instead of adding yardage.

Fault: The two most common errors are holding the right elbow too far away from the body (1), as the golfer thinks this makes a bigger turn, and collapsing the left arm to get the clubhead past parallel at the top of the backswing (2), again thinking this helps them generate more clubhead speed. Both of these positions result in an "over the top" move, causing the club to travel across the target line and finish low across the body (3).

1

2

3

Cure: Make sure that the right arm stays in a position perpendicular to the ground at the top of the backswing (4). The left arm must be fully extended to create tightness in the torso. This tightness or coil is called torque (5).

This position will help the right arm drop down into a good preimpact position (6), ensuring that the clubhead travels down the target line through impact (7). Work on this move and you will gain more power while keeping your accuracy.

4

5

6

7

# Weight Shift

There is so much confusion regarding weight shift on the downswing that it needs explaining in detail. Weight shift is one of the key movements in the golf swing. It determines clubhead path and clubhead speed through impact. If you do not understand weight shift, you are going to lose both power and direction in your swing.

Fault: Starting the weight shift with a rotation of the hips. When you start the downswing with a rotation of the hips

instead of a lateral movement (1), the shoulders immediately follow the direction of the hips. This causes the shoulders to open too soon, throwing the clubhead outside the hands, which causes the clubhead path to cut across the ball, resulting in both power and direction loss (2).

Fault: Starting the weight shift with a sway to the right. Sometimes in an attempt to transfer the weight correctly, the golfer makes an exaggerated lateral slide of the

1

2

3

4

5

6

hips (3). Although this does get the weight across to the front side, it causes the upper body to also move forward (4). Now the upper body is ahead of the ball at impact, leaving the clubface wide open, causing loss of power and direction. Usually a huge slice or even a shank can occur.

Fault: No weight shift at all. With no weight shift at all, the weight obviously stays on the back foot (5), causing the back shoulder to drop, the shoulders also open up, and the clubhead to cut across the ball (6). This is common with beginner golfers, and is a subconscious attempt to get the ball up into the air. There is very little power in this type of swing.

Cure: Shift the weight correctly. Move the weight across from the back foot to the front foot with a "slight" lateral movement of the hips, making sure that they stay square until the weight is all on the front foot and the back heel is slightly off the ground (7). If the heel is still flat, you have not transferred the weight correctly. This automatically retains the angle between the left forearm and the shaft of the club (for right-handed golfers). The clubhead will release with maximum speed and you will keep the clubhead moving along the correct path through impact, producing a powerful and straight shot (8).

7

8

# *Shanking*

The shank is the most dreaded shot in golf. Once you start shanking, it is almost like a virus, and it will penetrate the very depths of your psyche.

Fault: The impact position of the ball is off the hosel of the club instead of the clubface, causing the ball to travel of-line at 90 degrees to the intended target line of flight. A shank is caused by one of two things: The hands move too far away from the body on the downswing (1), throwing the clubhead outside the hands and allowing the hosel to hit the ball first (2).

1

2

The other reason for shanking is starting the clubhead too much from the inside on the downswing and not releasing the hands (3).

Cure: Address your ball after you have placed a second ball just outside of it (4). The object is to miss the outside ball while hitting the inside ball. This forces you to keep the club on an inside path, which will prevent you from shanking.

**3**

**4**

# Errors in Pitching

There tend to be more errors in the short game than in the long game. When most amateurs go to the driving range to practice, they feel that they must work on their full swing to get their money's worth. Also, a lot of golfers find practicing their short game tedious and boring. And, of course, if you are not very good at the short game, it can also be frustrating. Touring professionals spend over 50 percent of their practice time on the short game. Pros can chip, pitch, and get the ball out of sand close enough for one putt most of the time, but this does not happen by luck, only by extremely hard practice. As Gary Player once said, "The harder I practice, the luckier I get!" Short game guru Dave Peltz says that if an 18 handicap improved his short game from 50 yards to the level of a scratch player, his handicap would plummet to 9. This should be great incentive for every high handicap golfer to work hard on their short game in order to reduce their handicap. You can work on chipping and putting at home, so for those who have hectic

1

2

schedules, there is no excuse not to practice your short game for fifteen or twenty minutes, three times a week. As long as you are working with a purpose and understand your ultimate goals, these practice sessions should be fruitful.

Fault: The infamous "chicken wing," or collapsing left arm. Collapsing the left arm causes more bad shots in pitching than any other fault (see 1 on previous page). As there is a tendency to try and lift the ball into the air instead of allowing the loft of the club to do the work, the left arm will inevitably "chicken wing" and a sculled shot will result. The left arm needs to be perfectly straight at the finish.

3

Cure: Practice keeping your left arm straight through the hitting area and finish with both arms extended out in front of you (2 and 3). If your left arm is not straight at this point, extend it out until it is before you attempt the next shot. By working toward this finish position, you will ensure that your left arm stays straight throughout the shot.

Fault: Changing the spine angle. Golfers commonly refer to this as "lifting the head" (4). However, the problem actually occurs with the spine angle. As the head is attached to the spine, it looks like the head is lifting. This straightening of the

4

spine angle is again caused by a subconscious attempt to try and lift the ball into the air. The golfer does not trust the loft of the club to do the work and in an attempt to give the ball higher flight, he lifts up his upper body and a sculled shot results.

Cure: Practice hitting pitch shots waiting for your right shoulder to get to your chin, allowing your head to rotate or your body to straighten.

Fault: Starting the downswing with the arms. If you have a tendency to hit your pitch shots heavy (behind the ball) then you are probably starting the downswing

with your arms instead of allowing your torso to control this shot (5). From the top of the backswing, the first movement of the pitch shot is getting the left side out of the way fairly quickly, keeping the body ahead of the arms and arms ahead of the clubhead. This ensures that the hands will pass the ball before the clubhead.

Cure: Take your golf stance and practice tossing a ball underhand (see 6 on following page). To throw the ball any distance you have to turn your left hip out of the way and your hand holding the ball must travel toward the target (see 7 on following page). This is the same motion required for a good pitch shot. Now take your club and practice attaining the same feeling. Hitting the ground behind the ball will become a thing of the past.

Fault: Following through around the body. Very often in an attempt to clear the left side, the follow-through ends up around the body causing the shot to be pulled to the left (see 8 on following page). Obviously the pitch shot is an accuracy shot, so it is no good getting the distance you want in the air, but being 10 or 15 yards off-line to the left of your target.

5

6

7

9

10

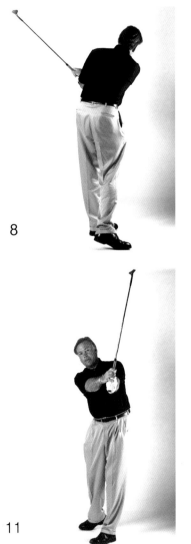

8

11

Cure: Again, the underhand toss drill (6 and 7) is appropriate, giving you the feeling of your hands traveling directly through to the target. At the end of the swing, your hands should finish in front of your chest, with the club shaft vertical (9).

Fault: Scooping. This is another attempt by the golfer to help the ball up into the air. A scooping motion of the right hand forces the left wrist to cup, keeping the clubface open and producing a sculled shot or a shot that flies fairly high, coming up well short of the target (10).

Cure: Allow the right hand to cross over the left through the hitting area, keeping the back of the left wrist flat (11). This rotation not only squares the clubface at impact, but produces the correct loft. This will also help to improve your distance control.

# Errors in Chipping

Fault: Breakdown of the wrist. This is a common error in chipping because the golfer wants to help the ball into the air and the lower hand gets involved and scoops the ball (1). The moment this happens, the loft of the club is influenced and because there is now more loft than there was at address, the ball comes up short of the target.

Cure: Make sure the grip of the last three fingers of the upper hand is fairly firm. This helps maintain a firm wrist (2). When the chip shot is over, check the back of your upper hand to make sure that it is still flat. If you have trouble keeping the back of your upper hand flat, take a popsicle stick and tape it to the back of your hand. By practicing with this aid, you'll soon get the correct feel. Another helpful aid is to take an elastic band and wrap it around the top of the club and your wrist. If your wrist breaks down while you are chipping, you'll feel the tension in the elastic band change. Work on your chipping until you can maintain a firm wrist.

Fault: Weight on the back foot. Many golfers don't realize that their weight is on the back foot until it is pointed out (3). They have subconsciously moved their weight to the back foot in an effort to help the ball into the air.

Cure: Make sure 85 to 90 percent of your weight is on the front foot at address (4), and keep it there throughout the entire shot. If you have a tendency to fall back during the shot, stand with your back foot on its toe. This will ensure that the weight stays on your front foot throughout the shot.

Fault: Looking up. This is another fairly common error, and should be the easiest to correct.

Cure: Stay in your posture throughout the entire stroke. When you have completed your follow-through, you should still be in the same posture as when you started out. Practice this in front of a mirror to make sure that you are not moving, or get someone to hold your head while you're chipping.

Fault: Lack of follow through. This is caused by lack of trust in your chipping motion and anxiety that the ball is going too far—a shortened follow-through is the result.

Cure: The chipping motion is like a pendulum. A pendulum moves back and forth at the same speed with the same length of backswing and follow-through. The same motion is needed for chipping. If you practice chipping in front of a mirror, you can check that your backswing and follow-through are the same length.

Fault: Lack of pace. Again caused by lack of trust, the golfer rushes the downswing, hits the ball too hard, or decelerates and hits the ball too soft.

Cure: While making your practice swing back and forth, be aware of the pace of the clubhead (1 and 2). Look at your landing spot while doing your practice strokes and your subconscious will tell you exactly how hard to hit the ball. Be aware of the pace of the club moving back and through and when you are ready to chip, make sure you hit the shot with exactly the same pace as your practice swing. This will give you tremendous distance control with chip shots.

# Errors in Putting

Fault: Poor alignment. This is absolutely the number one fault in putting. Golf is a "sideways-on" game and our eyes are not designed to aim from this angle. When we try to aim the putter face at the hole, we get an optical illusion as to where we are aiming, and most of the time this is incorrect. Golf is the only sport we play "sideways-on." Imagine trying to fire a rifle sideways; it would not be very accurate.

Cure: To rectify this problem, put a stripe on the ball. You can buy small plastic devices from golf shops that fit onto the

ball and allow you to draw a straight line. When you bend down to place your ball on the green, aim the line on the ball at your intended target. When your putter is behind the ball, make sure the line on your putter is square to the line on the ball.

Fault: Breakdown of the wrist. As with chipping, this is an effort to help the ball toward the hole.

Cure: Apply the same corrections to the breakdown of the wrist in putting as for chipping.

Fault: Eyes following the ball. When our eyes follow the ball, our head moves forward, causing the shoulders to open, the putter head to be pulled offline, and the clubface closes.

Cure: Look at the spot where the ball was after you have hit it. Practice listening for the sound of the ball going into the cup before you look up.

Fault: Lack of follow-through. This is caused by a lack of trust and fear of hitting the ball too hard.

Cure: Practice hitting putts where your backswing is half the length of your follow-through. Once you have gained confidence in your distance control, you will not quit on your putts.

Fault: Lack of pace. The same pendulum motion that applied to chipping also applies to putting. The follow-through should be twice as long as the backswing, but the pace should be even back and through.

Cure: To improve your pace you could buy yourself a metronome. Set it to a steady beat between 60 and 70, for example. End your backswing on one beat and your follow-through on another.

# *Errors in Sand Play*

The errors in sand play are similar to the errors found in pitching.

Fault: Weight on the back foot. At the address position, the golfer tends to leave the weight on the back foot, subconsciously thinking that this will help him get the ball out of the bunker (1).

Cure: Make sure the weight is set on the front foot. Keep your weight on the front foot throughout the entire shot (2).

Fault: Scooping. This fault relates to having the weight on the back foot (1). The lower hand tries to flip under the upper hand, causing the golfer to hit too far behind the ball. The club bounces off the sand and the golfer ends up sculling the ball (see 3 on following page).

Cure: The right hand should cross over the left as it would in a normal pitch shot (see 4 and 5 on following

1

2

page). The left arm must be extended and both hands should finish in front of your body, with your weight on your front foot (6).

Fault: Left arm collapses (7). Another subconscious attempt to help the ball up into the air instead of trusting the club to do the work.

Cure: Make sure that the left arm stays straight throughout this entire shot (8). Finish with all of your weight on your front foot and with both arms extended out in front of you. Spend some time in the practice bunker until you can do this consistently, and success will be yours on the golf course with this shot.

3

6

# Your Short Game Handicap

This is a fun method of improving your short game that helps you recognize how strong or weak your short game really is. You want to keep score of how many shots you take from inside of 50 yards on any given hole. Obviously, on some holes you will hit the green from further out and there would be no short game handicap on that hole.

Reproduced here is an example of a scorecard for the first nine holes at Pawleys Plantation Golf and Country Club, showing how to calculate your short game handicap. In the first column, on line one, is the name of the player, in this case, Mel; next to this is the score and the number of putts on each green. On line two, "Drive/GIR" indicates where the drives went and which greens were hit in regulation figures. Line three has "CPB," which stands for chips, pitches, and bunker shots. On the same line the distance finished from the hole after playing the shot to the green is recorded. Line four gives the short game handicap.

| Hole | 1 | 2 | 3 | 4 | 5 | 6 | 7 | 8 | 9 | OUT |
|---|---|---|---|---|---|---|---|---|---|---|
| GOLDEN BEAR 75.3/146 | 511 | 461 | 194 | 543 | 390 | 432 | 172 | 452 | 416 | 3571 |
| BLUE HERON 72.5/137 | 495 | 441 | 170 | 498 | 371 | 391 | 151 | 419 | 387 | 3323 |
| WHITE EGRET 70.8/130 | 484 | 408 | 162 | 468 | 353 | 382 | 131 | 387 | 358 | 3133 |
| MEL | $4_1$ | $4_1$ | $3_2$ | $4_1$ | $4_2$ | $5_2$ | $3_2$ | $4_2$ | $4_1$ | 35 14 |
| DRIVE / GIR | L45 X1 | X6R | 5X | X25 | X7X | L75 | 7X | X6X | 3W80 | 5 6 |
| CPB / DISTANCE | P10 | C4 | 30 | B3 | 25 | B10 | 15 | 30 | C6 | |
| Par | 5 | 4 | 3 | 5 | 4 | 4 | 3 | 4 | 4 | 36 |
| Men's Handicap | 15 | 1 | 11 | 13 | 5 | 7 | 17 | 3 | 9 | |
| SHORT GAME HDK | 2 | 2 | | 2 | | 3 | | | 2 | 11 5 / 2.2 |
| YELLOW FINCH S: 68.0/125 L: 73.2/131 | 426 | 354 | 127 | 450 | 322 | 367 | 124 | 361 | 351 | 2882 |
| RED TAIL HAWK 70.5/124 | 395 | 314 | 125 | 419 | 272 | 366 | 124 | 286 | 310 | 2611 |
| Ladies' Handicap | 11 | 1 | 15 | 7 | 5 | 9 | 17 | 3 | 13 | |

Date: 1/21/2002   Scorer: _____   Attest: _____

On hole No. 1 the player's drive missed the fairway on the left, and he hit a 4-iron short of the green. He played a pitch shot to ten feet from the hole and sank the putt. The score is four with one putt, and because two shots were taken from inside of 50 yards, the short game handicap on this hole is two.

On hole No. 2 he hit his drive on the fairway (indicated by an x) and hit a 6-iron to the right of the green. He chipped up to within four feet of the hole and sank the putt. So the score was four with one putt, and because of the chip and one putt, the short game handicap on this hole is two. On hole No. 3 he hit a 5-iron on the green about thirty feet from the hole. He then two putted for his par 3. As he had no short game shots from inside of 50 yards, there is no short game handicap on this hole.

On hole No. 4 he hit his drive on the fairway and hit a 2-iron into the front bunker guarding the green. He hit his bunker shot to within three feet from the hole and one-putted for a birdie 4. Again the short game handicap is two. On hole No. 5 his drive was on the fairway, he hit a 7-iron on the green, and two-putted from twenty-five feet for a regulation par with no short game handicap on this hole. On hole No. 6 he missed the fairway on the left with his drive and hit a 9-iron into the greenside bunker. He hit his bunker

shot to ten feet of the hole and two-putted for a bogey 5. He took three shots to get into the hole from inside of 50 yards so his short game handicap on this hole is three.

At the end of nine holes there were five holes in which he played shots from inside of 50 yards, totaling 11 shots. Dividing the number of shots, 11, by the number of holes where he played shots from inside of 50 yards, 5, gives the short game handicap of 2.2.

If your handicap is between zero and nine your goal is to have a short game handicap of 2.5 average. If your handicap is between 10 and 18 your goal is to have a short game handicap of 2.75 average. And if your handicap is above 18 your goal is to have a short game handicap of 3.0 average. Start keeping your short game handicap every time you play, as this gives you incentive to work on your short game and become a wizard around the greens.

# Bad-Weather Golf

"When it's breezy, swing easy" is another true cliché. Playing in the wind can be daunting for most golfers, but as long as you play your normal game and don't try to overpower the ball, the wind is just another test of your ability.

## Playing in the Wind

In wind, play the ball further back in your stance and take at least one more club, maybe two, depending on the strength of the wind. Then just forget about the wind and make a good golf swing.

BELOW: *Playing in the wind.*

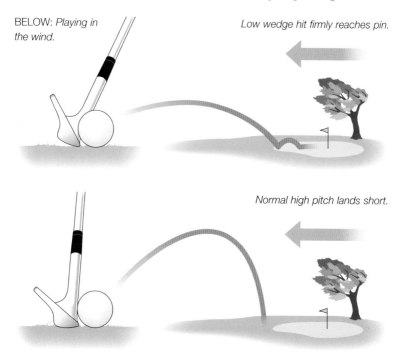

*Low wedge hit firmly reaches pin.*

*Normal high pitch lands short.*

When playing downwind, be aware that the ball will not stop as quickly, so you want to land your ball short of the target. The wind is also going to carry the ball further in the air so you want to use one less club, maybe two, depending on the strength of the wind. It is sometimes better to use a 3-wood off the tee instead of the driver, as it will get the ball up into the air and carry it almost as far as the driver.

When playing in a crosswind, take one additional club and aim to a target to the left or right of the fairway or green depending on the direction of the wind. Try to hit the ball directly to this target and do not make compensations in your swing to steer the ball back on-line.

### Playing in Rain

I don't know anybody who enjoys playing in the rain, but sometimes we are caught in the middle of the round, or, if we are playing in a tournament, we have no option.

Good rain gear is an essential element of playing well in wet conditions. A good rain suit that buttons or zips all the way up to the neck, and has pockets for balls and tees, plus a large, sturdy umbrella with a towel hung inside on one of the supporting stays will help keep both body and hands dry. It is a good idea to keep a pair of all-weather gloves in your bag for these occasions as well. Nothing is more disconcerting than feeling that the club is going to slip out of your hands during the swing. Carry all of this equipment in your bag if there is even the slightest chance of rain during your round.

Finally, like playing in the wind, keep the swing nice and easy. If you are playing in a tournament, remember that everyone is playing under the same conditions. You will also have to accept the fact that your score is going to be slightly higher than normal. Stay patient with yourself throughout the round.

# COURSE MANAGEMENT

Course management refers to decision-making by a golfer on club selection and the type of shots chosen when facing the various situations presented during a round of play. A person with good course management skills has the ability to make the right decision for any given situation. Weigh the risk and the reward of each individual shot and evaluate not only your skill level, but also how you are playing on a particular day. If you are not striking the ball well, take less risk. If you are having a good ball-striking round, sometimes taking a calculated risk will be to your advantage.

On any given day you may be playing your A game, B game, or C game. A is when you are playing above average, B is playing your average game, and C is when you are playing below average. On your A days, you can take a little more risk and play to a particular side of the fairway or play to tight pin positions. On your B days, play to the middle of the fairways and greens, and on your C days, play more conservatively, sometimes even laying up short of the green if there is anything there that could penalize a wayward shot.

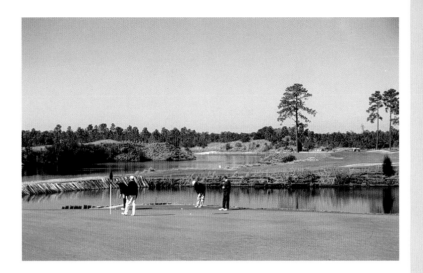

The first hole at Pawleys Plantation, for example, is a slight dogleg to the right par 5. The best place to be is on the left side of the fairway. You will be completely blocked out if you go right, but you can advance the ball fairly well up the fairway from the left-side rough or trees. Once you have hit your drive on this par 5, you must decide how to play your second shot. Can you reach the green in two? If not, put away that fairway wood, take a middle iron, and play safely up the fairway.

If you feel you can reach the green in two, be aware that the trouble on this hole has now shifted to the left, where there is out of bounds fairly close to the green.

Now it is better to err to the right than the left, so favor the right-hand side of the green for this shot. Missing the green to the right will still allow you the chance of getting the ball up and down.

If you have laid up with your second shot, you should now use a pitching or sand wedge for your third. Do not be complacent here. Focus as well as you would with longer shots. Be aware of the wind especially, as a high shot is going to be affected more than your last two shots. Take careful notice of the distance to the flag, not just looking at the distance marker, but to see whether the flag is on the front or back of the green. (This could

239

affect the shot by one or two clubs.) Then factor in the wind and select your club. Focus on this shot as you would your drive.

Consider the contours of the green as you are approaching it, as you will see contours from a distance that you will not notice once you are on the green. Look at these undulations both down the line and across the line to get a better feel for the break and speed. Follow these steps and you'll play your first hole much better. Focus for the rest of the round and your scores will definitely improve.

# MENTAL ATTITUDE

You already know how mentally challenging putting can be. An excitable player will have an impossible time on the green. The same is true for your play on the course. The way your mind works affects how your body responds. If you become irate at hitting a bad shot, your chances of hitting the next shot well are very slim. There are dozens of books published on nothing but the mental side of golf. Tour players have coaches designated to help them deal with the psychological torture a high-pressure, competitive round can inflict.

Golfers such as Ben Hogan, Jack Nicklaus, and Tiger Woods all have an amazing capacity for performing extremely well in pressured situations. Although these players were born with extraordinary skill both mentally and physically, the average player can train himself to be mentally tougher. By understanding how the conscious and subconscious minds interact with one another, the average golfer can learn to not get too mechanical on the golf course and to trust his swing when he needs to rely on it most.

Your attitude toward everyday life has a lot to do with how you react on the golf course. If you speed through traffic like an idiot, chances are you have a fast golf swing and have broken a few clubs in your day. Chances also are good that you have trouble enjoying your golf game. Remember that the game is fun and every time you have the opportunity to spend a morning or afternoon on the course is less time you have to spend working. So, don't make work out of your golf game.

# The Process

The golf swing is basically just a motor skill, and in order to learn a motor skill, we first have to do it consciously. Then, as we repeat that motion over and over, it will transfer itself into the subconscious, where it is stored as a habit, or, in the case of the golf swing, a series of habits. So the grip is a habit, the stance is a habit, the takeaway, and so on. In order to understand the learning process, it is important to understand how habits are formed and how habits manifest themselves. This is particularly important in understanding why we sometimes hit the ball perfectly on the practice range and then head off to the golf course and play poorly.

Habits are formed by repetitions of actions. These actions are recorded in the subconscious and when a situation presents itself to us, we will react to it based on our previous experiences. For example, when you walk into a room and see someone you like, you will almost immediately smile; on the other hand, seeing someone you don't like makes you feel immediately uncomfortable. Our subconscious recognizes certain people based on the information stored there. The subconscious then sends a signal via the nerves to the muscles, and based on our past experience with that person, our body reacts.

As another example, let's refer to the golf course you play on a regular basis. There are certain holes you often play well and there are certain holes that jump up and bite you almost every time you play them. As you walk onto the tee and look down the fairway, the subconscious mind remembers that fairway, that bunker, that tree, or that pond. Based on your previous experience on that hole, your body reacts. If you tend to hit a good drive on that hole, you will confidently pull out the driver, step on the tee, and make a good swing. Chances are the drive will go right down the middle. If you tend to play this hole badly, your visual image is poor and you might take a tentative swing, with a poor drive as the result.

People often say, "Why does my golf swing feel so much better when I make a practice swing than when the ball is there?" With a practice swing you recognize a nonthreatening situation and so the muscles are relaxed and your swing is relaxed. When you take that pace forward and get into your address position over the ball, your subconscious is now

243

receiving a different message. Based on our past experience with that particular shot, the impulse from the subconscious to the muscles will produce a swing that is either good or bad. If we want to improve our shot-making on the course, we first have to improve that picture in the subconscious. The easiest way to do that is on the practice tee. By improving the mechanics of the swing, you'll become a better ball striker, and by improving the use of the subconscious mind, you'll be mentally consistent, as well as tougher.

The practice tee is where we work on the mechanics of the swing, so we are therefore in our conscious mind most of the time. However, once we go to the golf course we need to leave mechanics on the practice tee and switch over to our subconscious mind. We want to think of where we want the ball to go, not how to swing the club. The way to do this is to use what is called a "clear key."

1

2

# The 32-Ball Drill

The 32-ball drill is designed to help you change the established habits you already have to the new habits you are trying to ingrain. This drill was designed by sports psychologist Dr. Cary Mumford.

Lay the balls out into eight groups of four. With the first four balls, you are going to be in mechanical mode—in other words, working on mechanics. You're going to be consciously thinking about what you are doing.

Take two practice swings without the ball, consciously thinking about the swing changes you want to make, and try to feel the new positions. After the two practice swings, go ahead and hit the ball, consciously thinking about your new motion. Pull up the next ball and go through the same thing again, two practice swings and hit the ball. Go through all four balls in the same way.

The next four balls are going to be hit in the clear key mode. A clear key is a key to clear your mind to prevent you from thinking mechanics while you're swinging. We use clear keys every day of our lives, we just don't call them clear keys.

For example, when you're driving along in your car, you are not thinking about driving your car. Your mind is on work, golf, and things to do. In other words, you are not thinking of how to drive a car; your motions are automatic. That is a typical clear key. Your mind is preoccupied.

That is what you want to do with the golf swing. Instead of thinking mechanics, such as "shift my weight" and "keep my arm straight," you want to block the conscious mind from thinking these things and allow yourself to swing subconsciously.

A clear key is a word or phrase that is used while you're hitting the ball. The definition of a clear key would be "occupying your conscious mind while your subconscious mind performs established habits."

Your clear key could be "Geronimo." From the address position, start your swing saying "Geronimo," to keep your mind from thinking of what you are trying to do with the golf swing. You are on automatic. Say the word "Geronimo" three times. The first Geronimo will take you halfway up your backswing (1), the second will take you to the top of your backswing (2). Impact happens on the "ron" of the third Geronimo (see 3 on following page).

**3**

**4**

If you are saying your clear key at the same pace, and the impact point happens at the same point in the clear key each time, then the pace of your golf swing never changes. You have exactly the same pace in your golf swing from the first tee to the 18th green. Of course, the other benefit is that you are not thinking of the mechanics during your swing and your subconscious mind is in control, producing a repeating golf swing.

Hit the next ball, going through the same thing again. Notice during the clear key mode that there are no practice swings; you're just thinking clear key and nothing else. You can use any clear key you like; however, there are two essentials for the clear key.

One, the clear key must be non–golf related; you don't want any words related to the golf swing. And two, try to match the rhythm of your clear key to the rhythm of your swing. If the rhythm of your clear key matches the rhythm of your swing, the pace of your swing never varies from swing to swing. Once you have finished hitting those four balls, go back to the mechanical mode for the next four with the two practice swings in between each shot, the next four back to the clear key mode, and so on through the entire 32-ball drill. The goal is to eventually learn to play your entire round in the clear key mode.

Experts say that it takes three weeks to change a habit, so if you do not have the option of practicing for three weeks, it is going to take longer. One more thing: While you're in the mechanical mode, stay focused on what you should be doing right and don't get caught up in what you're doing wrong. Don't try and analyze the shot when it goes left or right, fat or thin. Just pull up the next ball, take your practice swings, and hit the next one. It will take you several years to develop to this level, so be patient in trying to make these new changes permanent.

# Playing Within Your Personal Style

If you play golf competitively, it is also important to understand how to play within your personality style. Top players in the game today have recognized this factor and all try to "play within themselves," which means within their personality style. Although there are many personality styles, for the sake of this book, we will break them down into four categories.

1. Driver. These players are "the slashers" and are definitely bottom-line oriented. They play aggressively and tend to be risk takers, sometimes to the point of their own demise. Players that would fall into this category are Arnold Palmer, John Daly, Phil Mickelson, and Lanny Wadkins. All of these players have that swashbuckling style that endears them to the average golfer.

2. Persuader. These players are the talkers. Persuaders are fun-loving people who enjoy their golf and treat it as a social occasion, even in heated competition. They are usually talkative on the course and play their best golf when they are in a relaxed frame of mind. Players that would fall into this category are Lee Trevino, Peter Jacobsen, and Fuzzy Zoeller.

3. Analyzer. Analyzers are very methodical. They need a lot of information at their disposal before they can go ahead and make a decision. Golfers such as Jack Nicklaus, Nick Faldo, Bernhard Langer, and Chip Beck would fit into this

category. These are usually the slow players and will sometimes be warned about slow play from time to time.

4. Craftsman. These players are the swingers. They have those syrupy golf swings that look like they are hardly hitting the ball at all. Craftsmen are the easy-going, laid-back personalities who often look like they don't really care whether they do well or not on the golf course. However, don't let this fool you, as these players are just as competitive as everybody else. Golfers who fit into this category include Freddie Couples, Ernie Els, and Retief Goosen.

Take this test below to find out what your personality style is.

Circle two words on each line that best describe your personality, going across horizontally until you have finished all fifteen lines. Add up the number of words you have circled in columns A, B, C, and D, and fit them onto the grid as indicated below.

| A | B | C | D |
|---|---|---|---|
| All business | Bold | Personable | Deliberate |
| Organized | Revealing | Courteous | Listening |
| Industrious | Independent | Congenial | Cooperative |
| No nonsense | Decided | Talkative | Reflective |
| Serious | Determined | Warm | Careful |
| To the point | Risk taker | Amiable | Moderate |
| Practical | Aggressive | Empathetic | Passive |
| Composed | Dogmatic | Emotional | Thorough |
| Focused | Assertive | Friendly | Patient |
| Methodical | Assured | Sincere | Cautious |
| Stoic | Definite | Sociable | Precise |
| Diligent | Firm | Outgoing | Particular |
| Systematic | Insistent | Fun-loving | Reasonable |
| Formal | Confident | Expressive | Hesitant |
| Persevering | Forceful | Trusting | Restrained |

Put your score from column A on line A, your score from column B on line B, your score from column C on line C, and your score from column D on line D. Then join the marks to form a square.

The biggest quadrant is your dominant style and the next biggest quadrant is your backup style.

Once you have identified your own personality style from this list, use one of the players mentioned as a role model, not necessarily for the way that they swing the club, but for how they approach the game. Playing within your style will definitely help you become a better player.

GOLF SKILLS

250

**B**

```
                                              15|
                                              14|
                                              13|
                                              12|
                                              11|
                                              10|
                                              09|
    DRIVER                                    08|          PERSUADER
                                              07|
                                              06|
                                              05|
                                              04|
                                              03|
                                              02|
                                              01|
A  15,14,13,12,11,10,09,08,07,06,05,04,03,02,01,0,01,02,03,04,05,06,07,08,09,10,11,12,13,14,15  C
                                              01|
                                              02|
                                              03|
                                              04|
                                              05|
                                              06|
                                              07|
    ANALYZER                                  08|          CRAFTSMAN
                                              09|
                                              10|
                                              11|
                                              12|
                                              13|
                                              14|
                                              15|
```

**D**

# Some Key Points to Remember

• One of the things that separates the elite players from the good players is their ability to keep it together mentally on the course.

• Realize that you're playing golf for fun. No matter what your score, remember that the world is not going to end.

• It's tough enough to swing with tempo and efficiency in the calmest situations. Anger only compounds the likelihood of poor golf shots.

• Not only will your game suffer with frustration, but your playing partners will become agitated with your outward expressions of anger.

• Be realistic in your expectations. Stay in your comfort zone. For example, don't hit a driver off the fairway if you feel you can't execute it.

• Never give up. You're going to get in some trouble on the golf course, but you always have the opportunity to make it up.

ABOVE: *Visualize a positive shot. Ignore hazards and bunkers.*

# INDEX

accuracy 213–215

address position 9, 29, 36–38, 45, 47, 49,
70, 90, 101, 204, 231
errors in 209–212

alignment 10, 29–40, 43, 44, 207, 229

arc drill, increasing width of 68

arm plane 55

backswing 36, 38, 41, 46, 48–55, 56, 57,
58, 59, 60, 64, 65, 68, 69, 90, 93, 151

bad weather 236–237

balance 34

ball position 39

ball above feet 182

ball below feet 180–181

Ballesteros, Seve 10, 138

baseball drill 66

baseball grip 23, 24

Beck, Chip 249

bunker shot, greenside 17, 140, 144, 146,
161, 172, 183

bunker:
ball in back of 153
ball near face of 150
buried lie in 150
long pitch from 151

Charles, Bob 9

chipping: 17, 98, 99, 100–113, 221, 229
bellied wedge 106

errors in 226–228
fairway woods 105
practicing at home 113
setup 103
6-8-10 method 100
Texas wedge 107–108
3-wood chip 111

clear key 244, 245, 246

Crenshaw, Ben 10

Couples, Freddie 50, 73, 249

course management 238–241

Daly, John 70, 205, 248

downhill lies 176, 178–179

downswing 32, 36, 46, 48, 50, 54, 56–59,
60, 61, 62, 63, 64, 85, 90

draw 82, 164–165, 166

driver 17, 32, 40, 68, 70

Elkington, Steve 9, 15

Els, Ernie 50, 73, 249

fade 81, 164, 166–167, 167

fairway bunkers 146

Faldo, Nick 9, 11, 15, 249

flagstick, playing close to 148

flop shot 95

Floyd, Raymond 119

follow-through 47, 60–64, 80, 90, 91, 93,
186

follow-through, lack of 227, 229
Furyk, Jim 9

golf school, choosing a 12
Goosen, Retief 249
green reading 115
grip 10, 11, 23–28

handicap, calculating your short game 234
hand positions 26–27, 36
hardpan, hitting off 163
high shots 185
Hogan, Ben 242
hooking 198–200

interlocking grip 23, 24
irons 16, 30, 32, 39, 77, 78–83, 163, 168

Jacobsen, Peter 249

Kite, Tom 9, 15
knee flex 34, 209

lag putting 125
Langer, Bernhard 249
left-handed shots 134
lob shot 92
lob wedge 99
Locke, Bobby 9
lofted 96
long blast 158
looking up 227
Love III, Davis 70
low shots 96, 186–187

mental attitude 13, 44, 114, 242–253
Mickelson, Phil 248
Montgomerie, Colin 9

Nicklaus, Jack 15, 24, 50, 114, 119, 242, 249

overlapping grip 23, 24
overswinging 205–206, 207

pace, lack of 228, 230
Palmer, Arnold 248
personal style 248–251
pitch shots, scale of 99
pitching: 17, 84–99
    errors in 221–225
    key features of 90–91
    7-8-9-10 distance method 88–89
pitching wedge 98, 99, 100, 168
Player, Gary 9, 138
plumb bobbing 116
posture 38, 64, 65, 209
power, gaining 213–215
practicing at home 18–22
preshot routine 43–45, 69
Price, Nick 15
pull hook 198, 200
pulling 30, 196–197
punch low 94
push hook 198, 199
pushing 30, 201–202
putters 30
putting: 17, 114–137
    alignment 120

ball position 122
clock drill 137
developing feel 132
drills 127–137
errors in 229–230
grip 117–118
posture 119
push drill 127
railroad track putting 136
repetitive putt drill 130
strokes 123–124
tee 135

rain, playing in 189, 237
reverse pivot 207–208
rhythm 69
rough 110, 170

Sanders, Doug 205
sand play 99, 138–161, 221
    errors in 231
    setup 139
sand wedge 98, 99, 106, 140
scooping 225, 231
setup 36
shaft 55
shanking 219–220
slicing 30, 190–195, 200
spin 83
spine angle 34
Stadler, Craig 9
stance 10, 29–40, 36, 183, 209
    closed 33
    open 33

square 33
steep slopes 183
swing plane 55
swing, 90 percent 73
swing 46–69

takeaway 41–42, 47, 49, 56, 69, 76, 110
tempo 69, 70
32-ball drill 245
timing 69
topping 203–204
tree shots 188
Trevino, Lee 10, 249
trouble shots 162–189

uphill lies 176–177

Wadkins, Lanny 248
waggle and relaxation 38, 39, 41
water, playing out of 172, 173
Watson, Tom 10
weight shift 216–218, 227, 231
Weiskopf, Tom 9
whoosh drill 67
wind, playing in 236, 237
wood play 70–77
woods, fairway 16, 17, 30, 40, 71–76, 77
Woods, Tiger 15, 70, 242
Woosnam, Ian 9

Zoeller, Fuzzy 9, 249

GOLF SKILLS